ED SHENK'S

Fly Rod
TROUTING

ED SHENK'S

Fly Rod
TROUTING

Ed Shenk

Stackpole Books

With illustrations and photographs by the author

Published by
STACKPOLE BOOKS
Cameron and Kelker Streets
P.O. Box 1831
Harrisburg, PA 17105

Printed in the United States of America

10 9 8 7 6 5 4 3 2

First edition

Library of Congress Cataloging-in-Publication Data

Shenk, Ed.
   [Fly rod trouting]
   Ed Shenk's fly rod trouting / Ed Shenk ; with illustrations and
photographs by the author. — 1st ed.
      p.   cm.
   1. Trout fishing. 2. Fly fishing. I. Title.   II. Title: Fly
rod trouting.
SH687.S38   1989
799.1'755—dc19   89-4353
                                    CIP

Book and jacket design by Art Unlimited.

Fly pattern illustrations by Art Unlimited.

Portions of this book are excerpted from previously published materials. The author wishes to recognize the following magazines, in which this material was originally published: *Field & Stream*, *The Fly Fisher*, *Fly Fisherman*, *Garcia Fishing Annual*, *Sports Afield*.

This book is dedicated to all who love the fine art of
fly fishing for trout. Special thanks to my mother and
father, Margaret and Ralph Shenk, whose own
love of the outdoors was passed along to me at an
early age; to my wife, Tommy, who has
tolerated the likes of me and my great love for trout
fishing; to Stan and Arlis Krammes, pupils
and friends, who have constantly urged me to put my
knowledge of fly fishing into a book; and to
my daughter, Patricia Irwin, who transformed my
chicken scratch into legible type.

CONTENTS

CHARLES K. FOX

Back in the thirties we were beginning to think and fish to the tune of "Match the Hatch." Dry-fly fishing on this side of the Atlantic had finally gained a foothold.

One of the great mayfly hatches found on the large limestone waters of Central Pennsylvania was the green drake, locally known as the shad fly. It became an annual affair for a group of us to travel the hundred miles to fish this great hatch, usually around Memorial Day.

On one such fishing escapade, I sat on a log beside Centre County's Spring Creek and watched a lad not yet in his teens casting a small wet fly. The manner of his casting made me figure that he was from south-central Pennsylvania, for that is how it was done on the waters near Carlisle.

We talked without introduction, and as the great green-drake spinner fall began I explained the procedures and handed him a couple honey-colored Neversink Skaters, a fly that was my favorite at that time. The combination of hatch and rise was terrific; the young lad and I had a great time with our spiders and we each took a couple good fish.

Fishing seasons flew by. I decided to live beside a good trout stream, and it was this thinking that led me to purchase a long meadow beside the now-famous Letort. Once located there, I heard reports of a local master angler and fly tier named Eddie Shenk. A meeting on the stream was imminent; one thing led to another and the skater flies happened to be mentioned. We looked inquisitively at each other, remembering from years past our initial meeting. This second meeting on the Letort was the beginning of a cherished friendship.

Eddie has been asked to write a book setting forth his ideas, practices, and experiences, and thereby make a contribution to a rich fly-fishing heritage.

Many anglers agree that not all fly fishing is done in rivers and brooks – there is much of it in the printed word. You are one such angler or you would not be reading this introduction.

Good Fishing!

Introduction By
JOE HUMPHREYS

I watched as Ed Shenk dropped a Deer-hair Sculpin at the very edge of the bank beneath an overhanging bush that was nearly impossible to cast under: he pumped the rod tip twice, the sculpin traveled only inches then disappeared in a swirl, and Ed was fast to a heavy fish.

In the fifteen years I've fished with Ed I've witnessed this kind of event a hundred times. Ed Shenk is the master of the sculpin, the master of the Letort, and has mastered many other streams—limestone and freestone, East and West. He is one of the truly great fly fishermen of our time; he has fished for over fifty years and has been innovative and creative, with a commonsense approach to the sport.

It is only with experience and an open mind that one can hope to learn about and understand the complexities of the trout: its habits, environment, and the food chain on which it exists. Few fly fishermen have the experience Ed has. He has fished the Letort almost daily from his initial outing at age four, throughout grade school and high school, and on into adulthood. There is no finer classroom in which to learn, and none more challenging.

When Ed was a child fishing on the Letort, he was once asked how he had been doing. "Well," he said, "I caught a couple of dandy eight-inchers and some little ones." That boyish enthusiasm is still a part of him, and his good humor endears him to those fly fishers who know him.

The necessity to imitate the natural has brought forth a desire in Ed to create innovative tying techniques, techniques that have won him a place in the history of fly tying. The Shenk Sculpin, the Letort Hopper, the Letort Cricket, and a few others, are all fish-catchers that are standing the test of time.

What Ed Shenk has written in these pages is a lifetime of experience, hard work, and the wisdom of one hell of a fly fisherman. Ed is one of the best in the country, one that few can equal, and one I am proud to call my friend.

PART I

STORIES ABOUT FISHING

Chapter 1

THE EARLY DAYS

My love affair with little trout streams began over fifty years ago in the Cumberland Valley, and the fair Letort was my first love. Picture if you will sparkling clear water, bright green watercress and duckwort, the darker green of elodea, the odor of mint, wild roses, and honeysuckle. That's my memory of the Letort, a stronger image than that of its trout. Lest the memories fade and are lost forever, I'll try to put into words some of my early experiences, my trials and errors, my successes, and what the waters were like during those formative years.

Memories of fish and rivers are a part of fishing, perhaps the best part. It is great to be on the water watching the fly line unroll, seeing the dainty fly alight ever so gently. The anticipation of the rise and the rise itself are part of it. The trout, as he charges to and fro and is finally drawn close to be admired adds to the pleasure. But, in my opinion, remembering these things is the dearest, most treasured gift of all.

My first memories of the Letort were of kneeling on one of the wooden bridges at Bonny Brook and peering through the cracks at the suckers and trout. I was three or four years old at the time. I believe even then I was awed by the little stream with its crystal-clear water and the waving bright-green beds of water plants. It was a couple of years before I really got to trout fish. Dad was not a trout fisherman but loved to still-fish for suckers and such and use the long rod for smallmouth bass. It was the romance of trout for me, though, and it really didn't take too much persuasion on my part to get Dad to take me trout fishing. Dad tells me I caught my first fish on my own when I was about two, and between then and the time I was seven I had lots of fishing experience, but none for trout. But pictures of leaping trout in the leading sports magazines, *Outdoor Life*, *Field & Stream*, *Sports Afield*, *National Sportsman*, and *Hunting and Fishing* really fired my imagination.

I just *had* to have a long fly rod, and my first one was a 9-foot Bristol Hexagonal telescope rod. What a club, but it caught trout. My uncle had given me a box of English dry flies and a box of snelled wet flies for Christmas. Between bait-caught trout, which didn't come easy the first few years, I finally caught my first trout on a fly. It happened thus.

We were at Bonny Brook for some evening fishing. I covered a lot of water in those early days. I was along the stream opposite the Rice (later Trego's) farmhouse and saw the rolling rise of a small trout. Repeatedly the fish was making little slashing rises – at what, I couldn't tell you. I crawled on hands and knees as close as I could. My leader had a #20 snelled White Miller on it, and even though it was a wet fly it landed just upstream from the rising trout and floated toward it. It all happened in a twinkling: The trout took the fly. I reacted like any normal seven-year-old and heaved as hard as I could. (It took a second or two to find the flopping fish in the heavy grass behind me.) I admired my first fly-caught trout, a 6¼-inch legal brownie. How proud I was of that fish. I released it and watched the bright red-spotted brown dart back to the protection of the nearest bed of watercress. That was the beginning.

It wasn't too long after that first exciting episode that the same uncle presented me with a 9-foot Horrocks-Ibbitson "Columbia" fly rod. Boy, I was in seventh heaven. My first bamboo rod!

I won't bore you with day-to-day details of my trials and errors. I hesitate to call those years my learning years because I'm still learning. I really did apply myself with a lot of practice casting and a lot of reading.

18

As I fished, I watched some of the more successful fishermen, their approaches, and varied tactics. Most of these were bait fishermen, and to be sure I did a lot of bait fishing myself, but their varied tactics were such that I applied them not only to bait fishing but to fly fishing as well.

Hap Cramer and his brothers were basically morning fishermen. Piney Thumma did as well in midday as any of them and fished some at night. Day in and day out, the minnow fishermen caught the largest trout. Of these, Clay Gibson probably caught more trout over two feet long than anyone. Mostly he put in an appearance just as the last light was fading and fished into the night. He had located his big ones, so he knew just where to fish. He was strictly a minnow fisherman. Clay was a stand-up fisherman, and fished with a short line and a very long bamboo rod. I believe his close approaches were successful because of the time of day, when the fading light helped camouflage him.

Hap Cramer fished mostly with night crawlers and was great with the low, stealthy approach. I competed a lot with Hap because we both fished the upper reaches of the stream. I do feel, however, that he would have been an even greater menace to the fish if his terminal tackle had been lighter. One stormy afternoon he took three trout over 18 inches long in Trego's meadow, on one of those days when weather conditions were right to put the big trout on the feed.

Piney Thumma was a big man and another stand-up fisherman. However, he stayed back from the bank almost a long rod length and fished the undercuts and other hiding spots. Many times I watched him stand in one spot, without moving, for upwards of an hour, and many times he was rewarded with a trout.

Lest you think the Letort was strictly a bait fisherman's paradise, I will mention a few of the fly fishermen whose paths crossed mine.

Charlie Fox, of course, was one of those that I ran into on occasion. Charlie, always quite the gentleman, would have time to talk cheerfully with the little towheaded boy whenever our paths crossed. His "How are you doing, Whitey?" was the standard salutation, always asked with a pleasant smile. Years later, when Charlie bought a property along the Letort, we would cross paths more often and I have been "Eddie Shenk" to him ever since.

Another fly fisherman and fly tier, one Hoyt Brubaker, was my idol in those days. He was one of a small group of fly fishers who plied the trade on the upper mile of the Letort. His fly tying was great, and he gave me a list of materials and tools that I purchased to get started on a career of fly tying. I sure admired his flies, his tying ability, and his fly-fishing ability. At any rate, with all of these fishermen I watched and learned.

Since my early learning days were mostly on the Letort, I'd like to give a rundown of the stream in the late 1930s and 1940s. Why don't we start at the headwaters and drift downstream?

The stream itself is comprised of two main branches – very simply, the Right Branch and Left Branch. The Right Branch begins as a spring south of Pennsylvania State Route 34. This branch crosses Route 34 and is joined by water from springs in the Cress Ponds. These are by far the greatest water-volume producers of the entire stream. There are four major springs in this cress-farm system. After joining with the spring flows mentioned, the enlarged stream flows on for a few hundred yards and is joined by the Left Branch at Bonny Brook. The Letort flows north through Carlisle and past the U.S. Army War College. There are no major springs involved until the stream passes the War College and is joined by springs that come from the College and an individual farm. These enter the Letort about 200 yards upstream from Harmony Hall Road. The Letort flows another two miles and enters the warm-water Conodoguinet Creek at the village of Middlesex. The stream gradient is about seven feet per mile until it gets to a point at U.S. Route 11 at Middlesex where there is a limestone ledge that creates a small falls. From Route 11 to the mouth, a distance of 800 feet, the little river drops 35 feet through a series of cascades.

Dear to my heart were the Cress Ponds. The sparkling clear runs and pools harbored the world's most beautiful brook trout. As mentioned earlier, some of these brookies were crowding twenty inches, although the largest I ever landed did not quite reach nineteen inches. I probably caught a baker's half-dozen over 17 inches during the last decade of the brook-trout heyday.

The Cress-Pond pools were created with wooden chutes and walkways. The chutes extended into each pool and were the hiding spots of numerous trout. Basically the brookies held in the open but would dart under these chutes when disturbed. The occasional large brown normally hid under the chutes and only ventured out at night. If one advanced noiselessly toward these chutes and did not create vibrations or shadows, or one of the brook trout did not dart around and alert everything, there was a very good chance that a cautious brown would take a fly or whatever. Sometimes the reward would be more than I could handle and one of the leg-long browns would play me momentarily before the leader would part.

My largest brown from the ponds? Well over 6 pounds with a number more from 18 to 23 inches. I'm talking of hundreds of hours spent in these wonderful fish factories. It was always a toss-up at daylight on Saturdays whether Hap Cramer or I would be the first one to these spots. Once the fish had been spooked, it took hours before they could be fooled again.

There was a short meadow stretch of the Letort owned by the cross-pond people, about fifteen feet wide. This short stretch had some undercut banks, one overhanging mulberry tree, and numerous beds of watercress before it flowed under a wooden fence into another property. This property at the time was called "Rice's" and is one of the original William Penn Land Grants. The upper end of Rice's contained a footbridge. Not more than seventy yards below this was a low stone dam created to force some of the flow to the west bank, where it was channeled under a small building that housed a waterwheel. This covered pool, on occasion, housed a respectable fish or two, and of course was one of the hot spots never passed up. Drifting a fly into this pool from the upstream side was courting disaster because the wheel picked up the leader and would take an entire fly line if one was not quick enough to break off the fly. Sneaking into the pool on the downstream side made more sense, and over a period of years a number of decent browns and brookies were persuaded to take a streamer or wet fly. Popular patterns were the Dace Bucktail, Mickey Finn Bucktail, and the Hard-bodied Black Ant wet fly.

Not too far below the waterwheel the stream ran under a fence and into a pasture that, in later years, became known as Trego's Meadow. Mrs. Trego was a Rice and lived her entire life on this farm. At any rate, this pasture housed numerous belligerent bulls over the years, creating considerable handicaps every time it was fished. The great feature of this meadow was the overhanging willows and undercut banks. If there is one area of the stream that I have fished more than any other, it is probably this one. It was a childhood favorite of mine and remains so to this day.

During my early teens there were fourteen large willow trees along the west bank. Even then they were old, and as trees go the willow is fast-growing and becomes old quickly. Sadly, most of these willows have died, fallen, and were removed in years past. Efforts to replace them by planting willow slips is under way. The opposite bank of this meadow has had the same problem except that the east bank is a grown-up thicket, so the loss of trees has not had such a noticeable effect on the overall picture. These undercut banks and root systems afford many hiding locations for trout and is one of the reasons Rice's Meadow has always been a favorite of mine.

I believe I fell in love with the name "Bonny Brook" as well as the stream along this area. The name conjures up for me a picture of clear water, bright blue skies, the heady odor of honeysuckle and mint, and rising trout. Below the concrete bridge the stream splits with one small branch gliding under the last remaining waterwheel. Even now I can hear the little rumble as the wheel spins around, and the little *slap slap slap* of the water as each paddle is lifted from the water surface. At one time the pool below the wheel was over five feet deep and periodically would become home for various browns up to 20 or so inches long. The little pool is still a favorite of mine and every so often will furnish the excitement of a chunky brown, sometimes on a floating cricket or hopper, or maybe a Shenk Sculpin or my Flat-bodied Cress Bug nymph.

From here the stream flows under a small wooden-plank bridge that has changed little in fifty years. Just below this bridge the Left Branch joins the main branch and the stream flow increases. (More about this branch in subsequent chapters.) From here to the quarry bridge there are a few undercuts and overhanging grasses. This is a good sulfur section in season. A number of seasons ago there were at least five browns of 20 to 24 inches in the area from the quarry bridge back upstream to the concrete bridge. I know because I caught and released all five of them and could identify them as different fish. Most fell to a soft-bodied marabou fly of my design.

The very early days in this stretch, as well as in the rest of the stream, were tough ones for me. I had to learn, and mostly by making mistakes and scaring fish. I found, for instance, that once a trout saw you or your shadow the chance of a take was reduced nearly one hundred percent. So,

I learned very early to keep low and move slow. The sun at my back was an advantage only if my shadow did not fall on the water. Early morning fishing was great on the east bank until the sun came from behind the hill and forced my shadow to scare the fish. So, depending on the time of day, I might fish this meadow from the west bank. Mostly, but not always, the casts were short ones made to entice the fish that were nearly underfoot. I learned this close fishing over a period of years, and still practice it whenever conditions warrant. Many times the trout are back under the grass or bank so far that a floating fly drifted in tight, or a streamer fished near the surface, is largely unseen by them. Very close approaches insure greater success because one can watch the action of the line or the fly, and in some cases the trout itself as it swings out to engulf the fly, usually a nymph or streamer.

Of all the various sections of the Letort, the Quarry Meadow is the one that has changed the most. Up through World War II, the quarry there was owned by the Sours family, so the meadow was appropriately named Sours Meadow. At one time the water dropped downstream for fifty yards from the upper quarry bridge and made an abrupt left turn, creating one of the deeper holes on the stream. The stream then swung westward to the base of a very steep bank, followed it for a while, swung under a couple of overhanging willows, then continued on its merry way to the lower end of the meadow at the Reading Railroad bridge. Because this entire meadow was an open boggy area, it was probably the fly fisher's favorite because only a dropped backcast could foul up the casting stroke. Two of the legendary monsters of the Letort came from this meadow: a 10-pound fish caught by Rodney Glass in the 1940s and a 10-pound 8-ounce brown caught by Terry Ward one bright June day on a black Shenk Sculpin. This was another of my favorite meadows for a number of years. Over one half of this watercourse was changed when the present quarry owners obtained a permit to straighten the stream channel, fill in a portion of the meadow, and add the lower quarry bridge to ease access to an expanded quarry operation. From a fishing standpoint this was a trade-off because the quarry owners added over thirty tons of river gravel to the new channel and created additional spawning area that is used heavily every fall by amorous brown trout.

This meadow holds so many memories for me they would fill a book by themselves if I attempted to recite even a portion. I'll limit myself to three remembrances. The first occurred very early in my fly-fishing career, when I was still using the telescope rod. Not too far below the upper quarry bridge there was a particular brown trout that picked a holding spot and sipped incessantly from the insects that drifted over him. Many times I cast to this fish, as did other fly fishers, and, because of drag, I'm sure, the offerings were continually refused. The brownie would put up with this for some time before he would swing away and disappear. Ten minutes later he would be back in business again. At any rate, late one afternoon after school I approached the spot, made a pitch, and the little #20 White Miller wet fly was promptly taken. A 14-inch trout isn't to be sneezed at and I was proud. Very proud.

The second memorable incident took place in the turn-around pool. I was trying out the first hard-bodied ant I had tied myself. I made an upstream pitch and the line immediately was pressed back toward me faster than I knew how to compensate for it. It was one of those times when the trout wanted the fly no matter what and soon I was the proud possessor of a heavy-bodied brown trout. My first trout on a fly I had tied myself—what a memorable episode.

The railroad bridge pool was one that always seemed to hold at least one nice fish, and very often this good fish would fall to one of my offerings. I remember watching one tremendous trout under this bridge, a brown crowding 30 inches. Ed Koch tried for this fish a number of times, hooked him twice, and lost him both times. I used to peer through the railroad ties at this fish, but never fished for him out of deference to the few trouters hot on his trail. One morning we saw that the elodea beds were all torn up and the fish was gone. We heard that this monster was snared at night. What a shame!

Otto's Meadow began just below the bridge and continued downstream about twelve hundred feet on the east side of the stream. The west side of the stream just below the Otto farmhouse was called Scott's Meadow, named after the then-owners of the farm with its big limestone farmhouse (now owned by Bob Houser). About 200 feet below the railroad bridge there was once a brush dam and the third waterwheel. Remnants of the abutment for this wheel are still in place. The tailwaters of this waterwheel created a tiny pool that many times held a respectable trout. It was a tough

location to approach and fish properly. If I could drop my fly into the tiny backwater formed by the nearest concrete pier, and if the trout was quick enough, it was possible to hook a decent fish before the line straightened out and the fly dragged out of position. Early in my career I tried drifting the fly down under the wheel into the pool below. How do you stop a waterwheel once you hook it? Once, I lost half of a hard-earned fly line that wrapped around the wheel before I knew it.

The pool in front of the Otto farmhouse was divided by a larger concrete abutment that had a hand pump on it. It was in this pool that I initially struck up an acquaintance with Old George, one of the legendary giant browns of the Letort. This story is a chapter in itself and will appear in one, at the end of this book.

Otto's Meadow was home to some of the named pools. The Upper Willow Hole was just upstream from the farmhouse, where a gigantic willow tree and its root system protruded into the stream far enough to narrow the banks at that point. This hole remained until late in the summer of 1987, when a heavy storm washed the tree remains and its badly eroded root system out of the location. It lodged downstream about seventy-five feet at the concrete pier, which used to house the hand pump. The second pool was the Leaning Tree Pool, where a large white ash tree leaned out over the water. It was in this pool that I finally subdued Old George.

About 100 yards below the Leaning Tree Pool, the stream took an abrupt left turn, continued on for fifty yards toward the railroad, and then turned again. This was the famous S Bend, always a deep enticing pool of water and usually the home of a good fish or two. Since the bank on the railroad side of the stream dropped off abruptly into four-to-five feet of water, this is where we aimed our flies. It was a very good location for the hard-bodied ant, my first terrestrial. Bear in mind that during my kid days the trout season began on April 15 and ended July 31. Consequently, the cricket-hopper patterns, which normally reach peak use in August, were not in use. Earlier in the year, during peak "june bug" season, the fish were keyed in on this terrestrial. Surprisingly, everyone used a sunken beetle pattern usually a peacock-herb-bodied fly with dark gray or dyed-brown duck feather tied in at the bend of the hook and tied off at the eye. We used this weighted and unweighted. Some we tied with a soft brown hackle to simulate legs. Sizes were generally 12 and 14 because the june beetle is a large one. The S Bend pool is still a good one.

As the S Bend straightens out, the water from a spring enters the Letort, and this cooler water once resulted in a pocket of brook trout that found the drop in temperature to their liking. These fish could be taken in a number of ways, although they were never pushovers. Of course, in sulfur season they could be taken on top at dusk. Small streamers would work at times, and I always leaned toward the tiny maribous that we tied as small as #16. Often these trout were surface feeding during the bright part of the day and even as a boy I would use flies as small as a #22, which was as little as they came back then. One of my favorite dry flies was a #20 Wickhams Fancy, tied in England. I acquired a dozen of these at one time and if used sparingly, they lasted a number of years. I suppose the little gold-bodied palmer-tied fly suggested an ant or beetle. At any rate, they were deadly at times. We had long, stiff fly rods that made the hooking and landing of medium-sized trout on tiny flies even more remarkable by today's standards.

Below the spring at Scott's farmhouse (now Houser's) there was the second willow hole, long a favorite of mine. It was here that I fought a tremendous trout to a standstill only to have the barbless white marabou fly pull out after a long battle. This episode appears in Chapter 3.

Not far below the Willow Hole there was a series of logjams that made excellent hiding for big trout. This was always a big trout section because of the good cover. Just below the last jam was a massive wild rose bush beside the appropriately named Rose Bush Hole. Water under the overhanging bush was nearly five feet deep, always a favorite spot for big trout. During Japanese beetle days the bush would be loaded with these bugs, which made the spot even more inviting. I once popped a Letort Cricket over an excited trout that took in a hurry, and I became the proud possessor of a six-pound male brown.

Just below the rose bush the stream again sweeps left and then right, and we called this the Little S Bend. The stream flowed another seventy yards past what is now Marinaro's Meadow. The next meadow was actually a pasture field, housing a small herd of cattle at times. Once I watched as Professor Fink of Dickinson College fended off a small inquisitive bull with his 3-piece 7½-foot bamboo rod. (I could even tell you the make and model of the Professor's rod, but that really is immaterial.) This is what we called the Barnyard Meadow, which, along with Thorntree Meadow, is mentioned in Ernest Schweibert's *Legend and the Letort*. It was in Thorntree Meadow that Charlie Fox had his tiny Quonset hut fishing cabin. Although this area is closer to my home than is Bonny Brook, I did not fish it nearly as often. Occasionally, I would have a chance to sit and talk with Charlie Fox or one of his many friends. Mostly, I fished this meadow on early summer days after school was out for the year, and I seldom saw anyone.

This meadow had a couple of unique turn-arounds in it, always the home of selective trout. The stream at this point was straightened out when Interstate 81 was put in, changing the entire charm and character of the little meadow. It was here that the famous Jassid fly, developed by Vince Marinaro, was originated and christened along with some of the other tiny terrestrial ants: the fur-bodied ants and the Horsehair Ant.

The turn-around meadow glides past the famous Nineteenth Hole, where fly fishers met at the end of the fishing season for the "last supper."

The Nineteenth Hole was the place to visit if you came to the Letort to swap stories or associate with any number of competent fly tiers and fishermen. You might run into Ernie Schweibert, Jim Bashline, Don Dubois, Ned Smith, Keith Schuyler, or you might have been around when Vince Marinaro was taking some of his famous rising trout photographs. It was in this pool that Vince and the Pontoon Hopper played the gigantic trout "Vesuvius" to a standstill, only to have the silkworm leader part after many minutes of vainly trying to get this big fish into a net. I believe it was then that Vince decided that a large long-handled net would become part of his every-day angling attire.

This area is part of Charlie Fox's "Enchanted Meadow," and it contains some of the nicest deep water of the entire stream. If ever there was a representative meadow, it is this one. It contains deep holes, undercut banks, overhanging grasses, logjams, and overhanging trees. Over the seasons I have caught hundreds of trout in the Enchanted Meadow, and it is probably better now than it was thirty years ago. Again, like other portions of the stream, the emphasis is on stealth, accurate casting, and in the case of dry flies, a drag-free drift.

At the lower end of the Enchanted Meadow, Charlie has placed many tons of river gravel for the largest spawning area in the entire stream. Late October, November, and December see numerous excited brown trout using the various redds to lay and fertilize their eggs. Hen fish up to 10 pounds have put in an appearance here as well as males up to four or five pounds.

As the Letort passes this spawning area it abruptly turns right and then abruptly left as it flows into Romberger's Meadow. This is within the Borough of Carlisle and the stream takes on a semi-urban character. Being closer to home, this section saw me many times after school when I just couldn't spare the extra ten minutes to pedal my bicycle up to Bonny Brook. This is the last meadow in the special flies-only fishing area, which ends at the now-unused Reading Railroad bridge. This was a good fly-fishing meadow and in it I gained many hours of experience fishing the tiny wet flies, nymphs, bucktail streamers, and various dry flies. Of course my early days preceded the hot-weather terrestrial fishing we have today. This meadow, even with its urban atmosphere, is a very good hot-weather meadow. In passing I might mention that the Hard-bodied Black Ant was one of my workhorse all-season patterns. Sizes 12 and 14 were used most.

In passing, I want to mention briefly some of the other waters I fished in my beginning years. Some, like the Yellow Breeches, I fished quite often, while others, like Penns Creek, I barely had a chance to fish at all.

My earliest days of fishing the Breeches were Saturday-afternoon forays for suckers with my dad. This was usually a February and March adventure, but it did give us a chance to catalog various sections of the stream for trout fishing in late spring. We leaned toward the smaller waters in the upstream half of the stream. Such streamers as the Mickey Finn, the Brown and White Bucktail, the Black Ghost, and the Gray Ghost were favorites, and on occasion would get me a decent fish or two. One Saturday many years ago, I remember taking one 20-inch brown on a tiny white marabou. The following Saturday I took another 20-inch brown from the same pool: one of these was a male, one a female. Taking these two fish made a believer out of me as far as marabou effectiveness goes, and these same marabou patterns are still favorites of mine. Favorite wet flies were the March Brown, Hare's Ear, Brown Hackle Peacock, and Gray Hackle Peacock. Of course the Light Cahill, imitating the Sulfur, was my favorite dry fly.

Trips to Penns Creek were sparse, done mainly to fish the shad fly or green drake. Just seeing those great duns, resembling butterflies in size, was a thrill in itself. Locating a trout feeding on the duns was the hard part; getting the hungry trout to take an imitation seemed pretty easy at the time. With the exception of these infrequent forays, my early-day fishing on the great Penns Creek was nonexistent.

Fisherman's Paradise, a regulated fly-only water on Spring Creek near Bellefonte, Pennsylvania, was one of the early fishing locations that afforded me a truckload of experience. The experience came not only from my own trial-and-error, but also from watching other, more expert, fly fishermen as they tried various means to entice one of the legendary monsters from this mile of water. At that time we were limited to five trips per fishing season. Two fish over 10 inches could be killed. Once the second fish was killed, one had to check out and quit fishing for the day. The hours were from nine to nine daylight time. When we did kill a fish early in the day, usually one of generous proportions, we would hold off until the last hour to try for the second fish. Many times we were successful in that last hour, capturing a fish upwards of 20 or more inches. It was during one of these trips that I first met Charlie Fox.

Green drakes were hatching everywhere and the big trout were frenzied. The flies I had were basically small, way too small to come close to green drake size. Charlie gave me a couple large flies, including a buff-colored Skater Spider. I caught a few medium-size trout, which I could handle. Finally, the snout of an old leviathan engulfed the big spider. My expertise was no match for this monster brown and soon I was nursing a broken leader. But failures as well as successes are part of the learning process, so it was not all in vain. I found, too, that the various methods of line drift and retrieve are direct results of accurate casting.

Chapter 2

WESTWARD HO

For various reasons, I did not have an opportunity to consider a trip to the storied waters of the West until the winter of 1964. Now, twenty-three years later, I have had seventeen additional trips to my favorite Wyoming and Montana waters. To recite my experience trip by trip would be lengthy, repetitious, and boring. Instead, I would like to describe my first trip as a newcomer to western waters, what I learned and how I fared as an experienced easterner. I would also like to describe some of the waters I have fished on subsequent vacations, tactics, tackle, and flies.

The initial plan back in 1964 was for a family vacation of one month beginning the last week of July and extending well into August. The family included my wife Tommy and my children Diane, Sue, Steve, and Patty. I bought maps and read and reread fishing articles about the area waters. We planned our itinerary to fish in Wyoming, mainly the Green, the Snake, and the waters of Yellowstone Park. Of course, my main concession would be to visit various scenic attractions extending from Nebraska through Wyoming, Montana, back through Wyoming into the Black Hills of South Dakota, and eventually back to Carlisle, Pennsylvania, my hometown. From Yellowstone we would visit some of the areas of southwestern Montana so I could fish the Big Hole, Ruby, Beaverhead, and Madison rivers. I also wanted to give the Spearfish a shot.

Pinedale, Wyoming, was the first serious stop for fishing. I had read a Wyoming article by Al McClane, and the Green River piqued my interest. My son and I left the Pinedale campground a little after daybreak to fish the upper Green. Initially we used olive-bodied shellback nymphs, and by getting them down fairly deep we managed to catch and release a number of cutts and rainbows up to 14 inches. As the sun rose higher I found that a small Letort Hopper did the trick, again with very active fish up to 14 inches long. By midafternoon we tired of this so we headed back toward Pinedale, stopping at a little meandering meadow stream named Duck Creek. The overhanging grasses and undercut banks gave us some solid browns up to 19 inches with the majority of fish close to 12 inches in length. This initial acceptance of the Letort Hopper with the yellow or tan spun-fur body, mottled turkey wing tied flat over the back, and tan deer-hair head trimmed hopper-shape was such that the fly became my number-one pattern for western trips.

Heading for Jackson Hole and the Tetons was next on the itinerary with a quick cast or two in the Hogback River. Again the hopper produced a few cutthroats before we got to our camping area in the Tetons. The idea was to spend a few days sightseeing plus some fishing time for me on the Snake River below Jackson Lake. During the day, an array of nymphs fished deep were the trick for the Snake River cutts. Come evening the little hopper took on a dual role and, I'm sure, represented one of the numerous caddisflies on the water. One evening as the gloom of darkness was descending I saw some rather heavy wakes in a tiny side stream. I put on a large Fledermaus streamer and immediately was fast to an exceedingly strong fish. This prize turned out to be a 26-inch lake trout.

As we passed the Snake River and its cutthroats and golden-sided whitefish, I observed that late evening was the best time for the greatest surface-feeding activity. Of course, one should not overlook the possibility of a daytime hatch and be ready for it. I enjoyed fishing the Snake for a few days, interspersed with some picture-taking of the magnificent Tetons and the various birds and animals. I got excellent shots of the rare trumpeter swan, beaver, mule deer, and moose. The backdrop of the Tetons really added to the charm of the area. Now, after twenty-five years, I have more slides of the Tetons than of any other single spectacle. We broke camp reluctantly and headed north into Yellowstone Park.

I might mention that I was driving a new Volkswagen bus and was pulling a light folding-tent camper that slept four comfortably. Since my wife and four children comprised the retinue, we had arranged it so that at least two children would sleep in the bus on an improvised bed. It all seemed to work out fine.

Fishing Bridge, over the outlet of Yellowstone Lake, became the park's first test of this eastern fisherman. At that time, fishing was still permitted from the bridge. I watched as one 16-inch cutthroat was surface-feeding. "I could catch that one on the first cast," I said out loud to no one in particular. "Please do," came the reply from a nearby bait fisherman. I sent one of the children back to the vehicle for an already set-up outfit, one of my 5-foot 10-inch fiberglass fly rods with a tiny Adams dry fly already attached to the 5X tippet. One drop, a short float, and the fish was on. I worked my way to the end of the bridge, got near the water, and released my first Yellowstone cutt. I was sort of pleased with myself, to say the least.

We proceeded north along the Yellowstone, stopping to look at mud pots, geysers, and the various animals of Hayden Valley. As tourists, we had to stop and take pictures, too. Once, we watched a grizzly on the far side of the river. A little farther on I stopped and intercepted four bull moose as they were being herded by an energetic group of tourists.

Below Hayden Valley we stopped for a late picnic lunch overlooking the Yellowstone. I donned my hippers, and armed with my tiny rod, a #16 flat-winged Letort Hopper, and crossed fingers I worked some line out to cover a feeding fish. I might add that the #4 weight-forward line cut through the wind very nicely and helped deposit my fly on the water in the correct manner. I held my breath as a generous snout opened to inhale the fly. After a moment's hesitation I set the hook, and the fight was on. Shortly, a brilliantly colored 20-inch Yellowstone cutthroat was reposing in the net. Even though the regulations permitted three kept fish per day, I recorded the catch on film and released my prize. I was ready for lunch then.

My Yellowstone Park goals were to fish the Gibbon and Madison and to follow in the footsteps of Ray Bergman and fish the Firehole. In particular, I wanted to fish the Morning Glory Hole so aptly described by Mr. Bergman in his classic *Trout*. This water is closed to fishing now.

We visited Old Faithful and other geysers before we ventured to the scenic Morning Glory Pool, a beautiful, deep hot spring with its morning-glory-blue water. As Ray did, I witnessed the eruption of Old Faithful and studied the hot water before my family allowed me to don my hip boots and have a go at the Firehole water. I caught a few fish in the fast water below the Morning Glory Hole before venturing out to cast upstream into the famous pool. Once, while bringing in a small trout, a larger dark brown trout chased my catch until he saw me. I slowly eased into the water and cast to the far shore with the little Letort Hopper. I caught, then released, a double handful of small browns (seventeen) from 8 to 14 inches in length. I could almost feel the spirit of Ray Bergman at my side as I cast. Over the next few days I spent several more hours on the Firehole. My best trout, a 19-inch rainbow, fell to a hopper near the mouth of Nez Perce Creek. I fished other famous sections like Sentinel Creek, Goose Lake Meadows, Biscuit Basin, and Iron Creek, each creating its own memories. I remember the frustrating experience of herding a large group of fish ahead of me in the Goose Lake Meadows; the large brown bear peering in the window while we parked; and lunches on the road overlooking the meadows. Once, I cast in Biscuit Basin Meadows, rose and hooked a good brown. Looking around, I saw a dozen tourists with cameras heading toward me. I braced for a picture-taking session, but the tourists bypassed me. It was only then I saw a herd of elk farther out in the meadow, the focus of the tourist group's interest!

Because our campground was visited daily by bears, my wife refused to stay there while I was fishing. One day, while my son and I made the trip to Bud Lilly's shop in West Yellowstone, I convinced her to visit the Old Faithful complex with our three daughters. I needed new waders and some information about fishing on the Madison River. Bud and Pat sent us to the 9.3-Mile-Hole on the Madison, but Bud advised me that due to the brightness of the afternoon, the fishing might be slow. I stopped at a pull-off before arriving at the designated hole, crossed the stream, and fished the less-traveled side. I landed and released thirty-five browns with flat-wing Letort Hoppers in a couple of hours; three of these weighed over 3 pounds. They were the best hours I have ever spent on the Madison.

Back at the Old Faithful complex my wife informed me that watching

Old Faithful perform six times was quite sufficient. Reluctantly, we left Yellowstone Park for Montana's waters. The next planned stop was Alder, Montana, where I hoped to fish the Ruby, Big Hole, and Beaverhead Rivers. Naturally, historic areas including the restored towns of Virginia City and Nevada City and the famous Robber's Roost of the Plummer gang would be visited.

In Alder, we set up camp at the Alder K.O.A. I was instructed to contact Orville Kelly, reputed to be the fishing authority in the area, at the Alder Mercantile. Kelly and I made plans for an evening's fishing later in the week. In the meantime, he sent me just above town for an hour of fishing on the Ruby; and what an hour it was. Even though I'm a nut about beautiful sunsets, the fishing was so great that I couldn't tear myself away long enough to take a picture. It was a high-catch hour – I caught three fish over twenty inches in length. My little 5½-foot fiberglass fly rod really got a workout. The smallest Muddlers I had were the hot flies for the evening. Fish were rising to a dense spinner fall of sulfurs, but I was hitting so many fish on the Muddler that I never changed.

The Ruby Reservoir contains a fair amount of silt, and when the water is being drawn for irrigation the lower Ruby River becomes so cloudy fish activity diminishes. In 1987, the request for water was minimal and the stream was low and clear. This was a fly fisher's delight and I made the most of it. As I fished upstream from pocket to pocket I was moving and usually hooking one to five fish per pool, depending on the length of the pool itself. The hot fly was the hopper – sometimes drifting, sometimes skittered like a caddis. I caught fish both ways, all browns with a top of twenty inches. In one deep pool on a sharp bend I caught three powerful fish on a dark Shenk Sculpin, cast upstream and fished deep.

One evening Kelly and I headed upstream about forty miles from Alder. The fish were smaller in size but larger in quantity. There were a few whitefish and cutthroat, and many small rainbows. Kelly used a short leader, heavy line, and two wet flies, the Royal Coachman and the Ginger Quill. He popped the flies tight against the steep bank and started his retrieve. My fishing was mostly done with the Letort Hopper, #14. We alternated pools until darkness forced us to cross the meadows and return to the car.

I visited Alder on each western trip, and looked forward to at least one

evening with Kelly on every visit. Usually, we fished above the reservoir, never fishing the same area twice. Kelly had been a cowboy at one time and was able to point out various Indian locations and discuss local history. Someday I'd like to visit the "medicine wheel" he located way up the Sweetwater, one of the branches of the Ruby. We also hunted Montana "rubies" at places Kelly pointed out, as well as "wonder stone," a beautiful mineral very similar to marble cake in color. Once, while fishing, I hooked a small rainbow and a large brown trout grabbed it broadside and hung on long enough for me to net it; I killed that old cannibal. Back in Alder, when asked how we did, Kelly replied, "We caught lots of trout tonight but put them all back 'cept one. We wouldn't have kept that one if we hadn't been mad at him."

Kelly died several years ago, and I miss him. I'll never forget our times together.

I took a day to explore the Big Hole, motoring across the desert from Twin Bridges to Melrose, hitting the stream just above the village. My first good look at the fabled water showed me hundreds of rising trout. Nervously, I assembled my gear and began catching trout after trout. The only problem was, these trout were actually whitefish. This was somewhat of a disappointment, but I learned to distinguish between the whitefish rises and trout rises. The hatch really was a *Tricorythodes* spinner fall, and every so often I would hook a trout between whitefish rises.

One morning on the Beaverhead completed the stay at Alder. I caught a few trout on streamers, fishing in the brightness of the August morning. We moved on, heading toward the east through Bozeman, Livingston, and then back into Wyoming. We had to see Devil's Tower and Mount Rushmore, and I wanted to give Spearfish Creek a few hours of fishing time.

Spearfish Creek is a small stream running through the South Dakota Black Hills, so I expected to give a shot or two in Spearfish Canyon prior to our first visit to Mount Rushmore. The creek was little more than a trickle because of the drought conditions. The tiny pools had many skittery but hungry trout. It was a "hands and knees" approach – a minimum of false casting and a delicate cast with the hopper and my Letort Cricket. The trout were not large, but they were peppy. One fish per pool was the rule, unless I goofed on my approach or my casting.

We headed home to Pennsylvania reluctantly, our month nearly consumed.

I have endeavored to try a new spot or two on the later trips. In addition to returning to the preferred streams of my first visit, I fished the Green River two more times. We often turned off at Rawlins on Route 287 and headed toward Lander, DuBois, and the Tetons. From Rawlins to DuBois we traveled through antelope country, an exciting animal to see and photograph. From DuBois we traveled upwards into the Wind River Mountains, stopping at Togwattee Pass for a breather, and then descending downhill toward the Tetons. Our motor drive West many times included an overnight stay in Lander before continuing.

Over the years, I have taken others on this western circle. My second trip was with Dr. Howard "Howdy" Hoffman of Chambersburg, Pennsylvania. We fished the Gibbon River in the park, in addition to the Pine and Snake farther down in Wyoming. Elk Meadows, on the Gibbon, has since become one of my favorite locations. The stream meanders so greatly that one can fish for several hours not a hundred yards from the starting point. As a meadow stream in August and September the hopper patterns are very effective here, along with the Letort Cricket. Again, my preferred sizes are small for western recommendations; go with #14 and #16 carrying the ball most of the time. Naturally, in a match-the-hatch situation we endeavor to imitate the fly that is on the water. In the Gibbon as well as other meadow streams, we would fish to the edges as much as possible, unless a mid-stream hatch was in progress; then, of course, we fished to the rise.

On subsequent trips with "Howdy," Dr. Tom Landis, and Terry Ward, we found the Trico spinner fall on the Madison River between Route 287 and the upper end of Hebgen Lake. What a thrill it was to watch the gulpers and wait nervously as they gulped toward us, only to turn away just as we were ready to make a cast. By the same token, casting ahead of a brown or rainbow, seeing its snout inhale the fly, and hanging on as the hooked fish went crazy, was an experience almost beyond description. I have taken such fish on small hoppers and crickets as well as the little spent Trico imitations. At times I have had to cast a just-under-the-surface nymph to connect with one of these babies.

Once, when I took Bill Skilton and Barry Beck on their first western trip, the spinner fall petered out and, before returning to the van, Barry peered over the edge of the bank where a tiny tributary entered the Madison. Instinctively, he ducked back and quickly knotted on a cress bug imitation. After wetting it in his mouth, he dropped the fly over the edge. Immediately the line twitched; Barry set the hook and held on as 2 feet of brown trout headed out to sea. "Ed, I'm almost out of line," he gasped. As the reel spool unwound, Barry pointed the little bamboo rod at the fish. The line tightened, and with a "twang" the leader tippet broke. We all exhaled for the first time in minutes. This was a case of knowing what to present, and how to present it to a particular fish. I know that Barry now fishes the West with reels capable of holding at least 100 yards of backing plus the fly line.

After catching thousands of trout, I don't find them as exotic as they once were. Not so the grayling. Even from the first western trip, I had the yearning to catch a grayling or two. One of the places to catch them is the Big Hole River above the village of Wise River. One of our early side trips from Alder was a journey over the desert, from Twin Bridges to Melrose and through State Route 43 upstream from Wise River a mile or two to a good pull-off. We fished upstream, taking whitefish, rainbow, and brook trout, and an occasional grayling up to 14 inches in length. Many times a small Letort Hopper or Letort Cricket would fool more than two dozen rainbows, some reaching twenty inches in length, along with large whitefish. The grayling rises were different, with many misses. If I hesitated slightly before I set the hook, my percentage of hooked grayling would increase. This was one of the few times when I grumbled if a twenty-inch rainbow was tail-walking across the water. One cannot catch a grayling with another fish on the line.

I spent time on the wide Missouri my last few trips West. The area below the power dams between Townsend and Great Falls is where I have done some of my greatest fishing. As Gary LaFontaine wrote in "The Missouri Nobody Knows" (*Fly Fisherman magazine*), fishing in this area is akin to fishing a giant spring creek. The late August and September fishing is either to the Trico, various caddisflies, or Diptera, large and small. Last year, for instance, the trout deserted the Trico spinner and keyed in on midge pupae and an occasional adult midge. I found I could fool these bulging fish on a #16 or a #18 midge pupa. I had to use at least a 5X tippet, and on occasion a 6X, in order to get adequate results. When a fish would start keying in on the adults I had to go to a #22 dry for best results. A fast-charging 20- to 22-inch brown or rainbow on a #22 and 6X is a thrill in itself, and going the distance gave a real sense of accomplishment. However, the hook would often pull out, or the tippet would break; so, as with most of my fishing, I mainly used my 6½-foot graphite rods with 3-weight lines, and seldom felt under-gunned. Occasionally, I used one of my favorite bamboo rods, my T-and-T 1-piece 6-footer, or the little Orvis 1-piece "Superfine" bamboo so dear to my heart. I have gotten away from the little fiberglass rods I used on my first couple trips.

I have had memorable trips to these and other waters with many friends, mixing sightseeing and fishing. One trip, Don and Lou Morrow, Stan and Arlis Krammes, and my wife and I plied the waters of Yellowstone Park, fished the Trico on the Madison, experienced good surface activity on the Ruby, and shared a rainy morning on the Upper Big Hole. The group's favorite fishing was with the Letort Cricket and the Letort Hopper, and everyone performed in a satisfactory manner.

On another trip with Stan and Arlis and my wife, we extended our fishing to some of the Glacier Park waters, as well as taking our first short taste of the Missouri. I have had several forays with Stan Krammes. On one visit, we included Doctors Landis and Hoffman; on the last one, "Speed" Ebersole and Roy Stephens rounded out the foursome.

Chapter 3

HITS AND MISSES

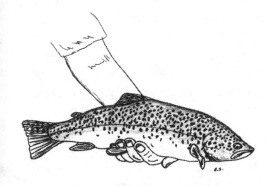

There are lessons to be learned with each fishing experience, and I hope these hit and miss experiences of memorable trout fishing will provide some lessons. Of course, the misses are fish lost and the hits are fish landed, although some were released. The following are only some of the many memorable fish I have encountered over the years.

Record Rainbow

The Allenberry section of the Yellow Breeches has been noted first as a fly-fishing-only section of water, and, secondly, a catch-and-release fly-fishing section, with one twenty-inch fish that may be kept per day. Recently, it has become a strictly no-kill catch-and-release area. It is during this second phase that the following episode took place.

The trout above Allenberry Dam take up their feeding positions around dusk and continue sipping minute insects until well after dark. I have to be in a particular mood to fish midges, and I plan to add 5X and 6X tippets and one of my favorite midge patterns well in advance of dusk. A few years ago in late April, I entered the water below Allenberry Dam about 6 P.M., too early for the midging fish to be feeding. I fished the water below the falls with a sculpin pattern to no avail. About 7 P.M. it was time to prepare for the pretty fishing. I tied on a long length of pre-used 5X, which hung from my lambskin fly holder. It was attached to a #14 Shenk Cress Bug, so I proceeded to fish back toward the Allenberry side with the Cress Bug before I tied on the 6X and a #22 No Name. As I approached the fast-water chute below the dam, I made one last cast. The nymph drifted along the edge formed by the slow water meeting the freshwater – a likely drift to entice a feeding fish. My line paused, I struck back; the rod doubled over and a heavy fish quickly dove toward the dam. Twenty minutes later I still had not seen the fish. "Smallmouth," I muttered to myself, for this tactic was typical of a heavy smallmouth. Briefly, my epoxy splice connection passed through my tip-top, so I knew the fish was getting tired. I gasped as a gigantic rainbow came into view. The fish was so deep that I miscalculated its length and weight. I clasped the monster against my wader leg and laid the rod alongside the fish; the length went from rod butt to nearly two inches above the butt guide. This fish was a beautiful full-color female, with no broken fins or blemishes. For more than a minute I held this great fish, debating whether to keep it for the wall or release it. Presently, the trout revived itself enough to swim away from my grasp and I pulled on the 5X tippet to bring it back, but the 5X tippet parted and my debate was over. The fish escaped. I measured the rod at 28½ inches when I got home. Two weeks later another fisherman killed a 28½-inch rainbow from this pool that weighed slightly over 10½ pounds. This rainbow held the state record for a number of years. Oh well!

The Spotlight Trout

During the peak of the Sulfur hatch on the Letort, I could usually be found somewhere on the upper reaches of this little river. As dusk lengthened into dark, I would proceed downstream toward the car. Most evenings I would scare a large fish. The fish would turn downstream, pushing a wave ahead of it. After a few nights I removed the 5X tippet and tied on a streamer, then proceeded to the hot spot, keeping low. After one cast it was generally the same. The great wave would start downstream and disappear under the little bridge. It finally dawned on me that I was silhouetted against the western sky as I approached, no matter how low I crouched.

One night, instead of heading for home, I tried another big fish. After an hour of unsuccessful effort, I headed for the car. I had to cross a little wooden bridge, so on impulse I cast the spot of my flashlight a few feet up the bridge. Lying in the light was a very respectable trout, not moving a fin. Now, night-fishing and flashlights are supposed to be enemies but apparently the trout hadn't read this. On impulse, I dropped my big, juicy Fledermaus streamer in front of the fish and jiggled it up and down, keeping the light on the fish. Without hesitation, the trout inhaled the big fly and was hooked. Presently I released a heavy-bodied brown nearly 23 inches long.

Two For Two

There's more to fly fishing than keeping count, although at times I have done just that; one night in particular comes to mind. There was a particularly large trout residing in one of the little pools in the upper Letort. I knew where the fish "held" when he came out at dusk, so I proceeded to the pool, eased into position, and made one cast with the #10 Letort Cricket. I could see the rather large fly silhouetted against the fading light in the western sky; I watched the imitation drift less than two feet and get sucked under with an audible slurp. At this point, most beginners (and some more advanced) blow it by overreacting and pulling the fly out of the fish's mouth or breaking the tippet. In this case, a lifting of the rod sank the large barbless hook in the jaw of the big trout. My tiny flashlight soon revealed an agitated hook-jawed brown nearly 23 inches long. The fish was gently released and slowly swam from sight into the darkness. I reeled in and retraced my steps to the car, but instead of quitting I continued on to the lair of another rather large brown.

I used a different tactic on this fish, one I previously used under similar circumstances at night. I eased in about twenty feet above the fish's lair, keeping low and treading softly. I cast slightly to the side of where I thought the fish would be holding and, keeping my rod tip high, allowed the fly to swing in toward the bank. I held the fly in one position for about thirty seconds, then slowly eased it back toward me about a foot. Allowing

the fly to drop back downstream for two feet by lowering the rod tip, I slowly skimmed the fly back toward me for several feet and then repeated the procedure.

The fifth time I did this I heard a tremendous "glurp." A few powerful runs and some surface commotion and this fish was ready for landing and release. Once again my tiny flashlight revealed a hook-jawed brown nearly 23 inches long—almost an exact replica of the other trout.

Night Surprise

This little Letort episode ended nearly as quickly as it began; however, there is a lesson to be learned from it. It was early June and I had finished a successful day on the upper Yellow Breeches. It was one of the rare times when there are so many March Brown duns on the water that the usually recalcitrant fish were slashing and slurping with reckless abandon. A #12 Adams did the trick, and nearly every fish cast to was hooked.

It was past dusk when I drove down Bonny Brook Road to the Letort. I had decided to fish the Quarry Meadow with a large Fledermaus streamer, one of my favorite night patterns. However, I made a very costly mistake: I clinch-knotted the big fly to a 3X leader.

For some reason the trout were not responding well and I was more than halfway through the meadow with only two small trout caught and released. I came to one section where the water was deep against the bank and the tall meadow grass hung out over the water, forming a tunnel of sorts. My fly hit away from the bank and swung in against the grass. Instantly, the fly was engulfed so forcefully that the ensuing splash and swirl was four feet in width, and my fly was torn from the fragile leader. I reeled in and quit for the night.

Three days later a fisherman caught a brown trout that weighed over 10 pounds; nestled deep in the throat of the fish was a big fly, the remnant of my Fledermaus.

Coincidence

Every so often, the water weeds on the Letort choke themselves and rot. When this happens they roll along, leaving the stream bottom very barren, and the trout are forced to seek suitable cover.

As I worked my way upstream in the Quarry Meadow, fishing every little nook and cranny, I came to a submerged muskrat den entrance and dropped the fly in front of it. There was a flurry of mud in the hole; I tensed, but nothing happened. Curiosity aroused, I placed my landing net over the front of the hole and stomped up and down on the bank. Presently, there was a "bump" in my net. I lifted it and discovered a plump female brown trout 17½ inches long. I did the same thing three more times that summer and caught the plump brown in my net each time. I never did get her to take any offerings sneaked in front of the hole.

One year later the weed was back, and the water level was normal. I cast one of my Letort Crickets along the same bank, got a tremendous slurping rise, set the hook, and saw a trout weighing 5 to 6 pounds on the fly. As I occasionally do, I eased up on the fish to reel in my slack line. This time I was out of luck because the fly drifted back to me minus the fish. I surmised that the hook stuck in a hard spot and never really penetrated the fish's mouth.

Another year passed, and rumors of a big trout, reportedly "three feet long," were passed among the fishermen. I heard the rumors and automatically cut the fish's size in half, chalking the exaggeration up to over-eager fishermen who, in the excitement of the occasion, have a tendency to see things larger than they really are.

This was the year of my sculpin design, and each time I fished the meadow I ran this fly down the overhanging willow branches without success. I showed the new pattern to Terry Ward, a friend from Chambersburg. He decided to fish the Letort downstream one June morning with the new sculpin, and upstream with one of my Letort Crickets; however, he never got the chance to fish the cricket because the sculpin stopped under the willows and was inhaled by a rather nice fish. Everything went right, and after a spirited tussle Terry jumped in the water and wrestled a 29½-inch 10½-pound female brown from the stream. Was this my muskrat-hole fish? I'd bet on it.

The Willow Hole

When you fish a stream like the Letort as long as I have, certain locations take on special meaning because of particular happenings. Such is the case of the Willow Hole.

The Willow Hole was one of those delightful little pools about four feet deep with a great undercut bank and overhead cover provided by a willow tree some three feet in diameter. Over the seasons many large and small trout were caught from this particular pool and I always approached it with the idea that a big fish was ready to take the fly.

In the first incident a snapping turtle, not a trout, was snagged. I had eased up to the hole, which was on the same bank as the undercut and the tree. A slight movement on top of the elodea weed bed indicated fish were present. I cast the large nymph upstream from the disturbance: the fly stopped, I struck, and nothing happened. I added more pressure, and the head of a large snapper appeared above water with my fly in his mouth. I did a hand-over-hand with the line and the dumbfounded turtle allowed itself to be towed to my side of the stream, which had an undercut bank. Now, a 20-pound turtle cannot be lifted from the water with a 3-pound tippet, so I reached for the snapper's tail with the idea of hoisting him up. I grabbed the tail, but in doing so had to lean forward. This was the right time for the turtle to head for shelter, pulling me after him. With nothing to brace onto, I was pulled head-first into the icy water. I came up sputtering and shivering, minus a turtle and a fly. It's the first and only time I was pulled into the water by anything attached to the end of my line.

Another memory of this pool involves a huge brown trout and is one of my "misses."

The August sun was still rising as I fished my way downstream and back to transportation. As I remember, I had fished upstream earlier that morning with the various terrestrial fly patterns, raising a trout here and there and even landing some. I switched to a white marabou streamer and fished only selected locations as I wound up the morning.

I approached the Willow Pool with the sun at my back, which enabled me to see into the water with my Polaroids. My eyes searched the water and I saw a huge brown trout slowly finning in a small channel between the beds of elodea. Without much hesitation I dropped the marabou in front of the fish. My cast was slightly short, and the fly swung harmlessly past the big fish. The second cast, some two feet longer, was on the mark, and I watched the big fish open and close her jaws, the fly disappearing. The ensuing battle was one of brute force, not a mad run. I turned the fish time after time, and finally brought her back upstream toward me. I could not get below her because of tree limbs and logs. I was afraid if I tried to get farther downstream I would be closer to a jumble of logs below the Willow Hole. The fish was exhausted, but each time I got her close she turned broadside, and the force of the water put so much pressure on my light equipment that I had to give ground. The fish rolled upside down with exhaustion at one point; this is when the hook pulled out and the fish slowly sank out of sight.

The following morning, spurred on by my sad tale, Ed Koch proceeded toward the same location. Before he got there, he saw a huge fish surfacing periodically, its big snout showing above the surface. The fish would go down and a series of bubbles would float to the surface. Ed cast one of my #12 Letort Crickets repeatedly over the fish; finally, everything meshed and the big brown was hooked and landed. When Ed brought the fresh-caught trout to my home that morning there were two things I recognized: a dark blotch on the fish's head similar to the one on my catch the morning before, and a fresh stab wound on the lower left jaw, right where my marabou had been. The details of this episode were recorded in Chapter 16 of Charlie Fox's book *This Wonderful World of Trout*.

The Stomping

Many times when I lose a particular fish I plot new tactics in case I am ever afforded a second chance. One particular pool in the Cress Ponds gave me a chance to try some new tactics. This particular trout had taken a big streamer early one morning, raced around the pool long enough to give me a good look, and then broke my leader by wrapping it around one of the wooden braces that supported the water chute.

I tried a few more times for this fish and never got a tumble. "What the heck," I thought, "this fish is probably feeding at night." I concocted a big, juicy "night fly" with a heavy silhouette. Putting this fly on the end of a fairly short stocky leader, I approached the pool just after dusk. Keeping low on hands and knees, I made a short cast that hit with a good splat. The bulkiness of the fly made a visible impression on the reflection of the sky. The night muddler floated a foot, and then disappeared with an audible *sploosh*. Setting the hook was an automatic response; the little 5½-foot fiberglass rod bent in a tiny arc and the leader strummed with the tautness.

My plan now had to be set in motion. Keeping pressure on the still-surprised fish, I took a long jump onto the wooden chute of the cress-bed flume. At once, I commenced stomping up and down, creating a noisy underwater racket. This confused the fish, and each time the bow of the rod indicated the trout was getting close to the boards, I stomped harder. This kept the fish from retreating underneath me and helped prevent the leader from being wrapped around any protruding planks or posts. Gradually, the pressure of the little rod tired the trout. Shortly, a brown trout 26 inches long and weighing 7 pounds 3 ounces was landed.

A year or so later I used the identical fly for some night fishing on Penns Creek, where it accounted for some very respectable fish.

The Crocodile

The largest trout it has ever been my pleasure to deceive resided in a spring-fed pond in southwestern Montana. One look at this huge brown and I nicknamed him The Crocodile. This fish was probably 3 feet long, nearly half that deep, and had the largest, meanest hook jaws I have ever seen on any trout.

Slowly it cruised the pond about twenty feet from shore. Dark and ugly with a deep salmon belly, many people thought it was a rainbow. But I knew better. I cast a #14 Shenk Cress Bug ahead of the cruising fish, watched as it opened and closed its jaws, and pulled the fly through the side of the fish's mouth without touching flesh, because when closed, his jaws did not come together on the sides. The unnatural movement of the fly caused the fish to disappear quickly into the depths.

The following morning I was crouched on the bank along the shoreline, waiting for signs of cruising fish to cast the cress bug to. Slowly swimming past me about ten feet away was The Crocodile. Who could fail to recognize such a fish? It was only then that I realized just how big this brown really was. I got the fly to the fish as quickly as possible, lest I let the chance-of-a-lifetime catch slip away. The fish inhaled the little fly and closed its jaws; I lifted the rod to sink the hook into its gigantic mouth.

"So far, so good," I mused, and watched the line slowly slip through the guides as the fish continued to cruise away from me. It's always a good idea to try to keep a big trout calm as he plays you or you play him. As more line peeled from the reel, the pressure mounted on the fish. Suddenly there was a line-sizzling run and the fish was gone. So was my little cress bug. Catching a 7½-pound minnow later in the morning did little to ease the sunken feeling in the pit of my stomach.

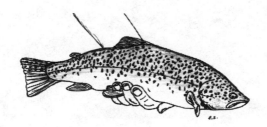

PART II

TECHNIQUES AND TACTICS

Chapter 4

The American
CHALK STREAM

Its Characteristics And Fly Patterns

The storied chalk streams of England and France produce some of the finest and most exacting trout fishing in the world. Did you know that their American cousins are every bit as great?

We call them limestone streams, or "limestoners" for short. Just as chalk is a specific type of limestone, so the chalk stream is a limestone stream. For instance, if the river Test were transplanted from England to a meadow in Pennsylvania, it would not be out of place at all; similarly, the Letort sent to England wouldn't cause much of a stir either. I once had the pleasure of being "gillie" to a British general on the Pennsylvania Letort. Being brought up on chalk streams, the general could drop a soft slack-line cast that kept his fly floating drag-free for an hour, while I had to be content with a two-foot "free-float." Normally, it takes a while for a newcomer to adjust to the odd, almost imperceptible currents of the Letort and sister streams, but the general took it in stride as if he were fishing the Test.

Volumes have been written on chalk-stream fishing by our friends across the Atlantic: Hills, Cotton, Walton, Grey, Skues, Sawyer, and others. They wrote lovingly of the Test, the Itchen, the Kennett, and the Dove, and in reading these volumes the dedicated limestone fisherman finds many similarities. The problems, fishing tactics, and even the somewhat easygoing attitudes are closely related.

When we write of the limestoners of Pennsylvania, New York, Maryland, and Wisconsin, we think of quiet, gentle waters flowing through small open woodlots. However, I write here of the big, brawling, rockstrewn rivers such as Penns Creek – a totally different breed of limestone stream altogether. Many of the alkaline streams of the West are chalk streams, as are the weed-filled western spring creeks, namely the Firehole, Gibbon, and Upper Madison; the Henry's Fork, Armstrong's and Nelson's Spring creeks are also essentially limestoners. There are many of these streams within our great country, some not very well known, but others quite famous. The late Ted Trueblood once wrote that there is no such thing as an eastern meadow stream. He went on to equate meadows with the great open-space valley bottoms of the West. The East, he said, had only "dinky" pastures. At any rate, meadow or pasture, they're all limestoners.

Limestoner waters collect deep within the earth and are forced upward and outward from caves and fissures in the limestone, starting out as full-fledged rivers. The result is lime-rich water harboring and supporting a great variety and abundance of insects, minnows, crustaceans, and trout. The currents are constant, seldom affected by drought, or rainfall short of a deluge. If a slow, steady rainfall would occur with an accumulation of two or three inches over a period of a day or two, you would probably see no appreciable difference in water color or height. Of course, a heavy downpour drenching the area in a short time would have a different effect: the stream might overflow its banks, the water becoming yellow with mud. However, even after such a downpour, in an hour or so the waters will recede and become clear again.

The following will compare the characteristics of the chalk stream and the limestone stream, the insect life, and to some extent the fishing tactics. Since I will elaborate on the Sulfur and other fish foods in subsequent chapters, much of what I mention here will be basic.

Seldom will you find such a pool as the diminutive Falling Spring near

Chambersburg, Pennsylvania, lest it be a pool formed by a man-made object such as a mill dam. This spring has a few natural cascades where the smooth-flowing water is interrupted by sloping drops of two to three feet. The Letort, on the other hand, descends at the average rate of only ten feet per mile, but drops thirty-five feet in its final two hundred yards before joining the Conodoguinet Creek. In other areas, the water flows smoothly downhill, broken only by the beds of elodea, a fallen tree limb, or various man-made obstructions.

Trout grow big and sassy here; because the streams do not freeze in winter, the fish continue to feed in the coldest weather. I have seen trout rising to midges (and an occasional Sulfur dun) in December and January in the Letort, Big Spring Creek at Newville, Pennsylvania, and Falling Spring. Strangely, these streams remain cold, even in the hottest weather. At one time the springs left the ground at a constant fifty-one degrees Fahrenheit, but temperature testing during the past few years shows a fifty-six-degree reading. Midsummer readings on the upper half of the Letort seldom get to seventy degrees, except in times of prolonged heat.

Weed growth in this lime-rich water is phenomenal; great beds of elodea form in an ever-constant effort to stem the flow. The relentless push of water forces its way over or through these beds to form channels and pockets of open water. These openings form the feeding and travel lanes for the trout; the weed beds create protective cover. This natural process contributes to the large number of trout per acre. As spring progresses into summer, watercress and similar plants extend above the surface to confine the stream and confound the caster. The presence of these weeds creates countless nearly imperceptible currents that make drag an ever-present problem.

British writers mention fly hatches, the abundance and variety of which seem to eclipse ours here. They write of the mayfly, similar to the American green drake found in our brawling rock-filled limestoners such as Penns Creek and its tributaries, but not found on our placid pasture streams. They also write of the Blue-winged Olive; our counterpart is much smaller and more sporadic in its appearances. The Pale Watery Dun of the Test and the Dove has its counterpart in the Letort Little Yellow Drake, or Sulfur. The caddisflies and stoneflies are not much of a factor on American meadow limestoners; however, they are prevalent on the chalk

streams of England. The Sulfur, little Olive, and the minute *Tricorythodes* are the important mayflies of our American waters. There are some lime-stoners of the meadow type that harbor a far greater variety of mayflies than I find on my familiar waters; however, because of this, the terrestrial insect becomes vitally important to the dry-fly addict. The lush grasses along the meadows harbor numerous leafhoppers (Jassids), beetles of all sizes, ants, grasshoppers, and crickets, all of which find their way into the water. Mayfly nymphs, cress bugs, scud or freshwater shrimp, crayfish, dace minnows, and sculpins all cohabit beneath the water's surface.

The phases of a typical season on a Cumberland Valley stream, as I know them, can become the basis for fishing your own favorite weed-filled chalk stream. Originally, I started phase one in April, the opening of trout season. However, since numerous streams are partially open to year-round fishing, we should begin in winter. Since the water does not freeze readily, and leaves the ground at a temperature in the mid-fifties, Fahrenheit, it is warm enough for the trout to feed. Even on the coldest days the fish can be caught if the angler can brave the elements. I wait until midmorning before venturing on the stream; fish can be caught on nymphs, either by sight-fishing to rooting fish or fishing the tiny pools and hiding spots, in hope of catching a hungry trout that is out of sight. If I cannot get any action on a nymph, which would probably be a cress bug imitation of my own design, a shrimp pattern, a larger attractor such as the Big Gray Nymph #8 or #10, or Polly Rosborough's Casual Dress Nymph, then I'll choose a streamer. My rule of thumb for cress bug and shrimp sizes is #14 and #16 if the trout can be seen, and #12 if I am fishing the water.

If the trout refuse or are indifferent to these nymphs, I'll use a streamer such as the Shenk Sculpin #8 or #10. I may vary the menu by using a medium-size Woolly Bugger, a leech pattern, or my little marabou minnow. All these streamer flies have one thing in common: a long tail made from marabou so the fly will appear alive even when it is being dead-drifted. I'll also vary pattern and color in the event that a particular trout gets wise to a certain fly.

On a chilly February Sunday, I took a quick trip to Bonny Brook. My wife went along to snap a few pictures because I wanted some fishing pictures with snow in the background. My first drift with a black sculpin brought out a brown in the 2-pound category. After nipping the fly I missed the trout, and he retired to his resting spot under a patch of winter-killed watercress. I rested the spot for perhaps thirty minutes and fished elsewhere. Later, I again worked the same sculpin past the fish's lie, with no response at all. My wife and I decided to give it one last shot before heading home, so I put on a white fur-bodied streamer with a long mara-bou tail. This drifted past the hot spot and was immediately fast to my old friend. The little one-piece bamboo rod quickly subdued the brightly col-ored male brown, a nice fish over 17 inches long.

During cold weather, trout will sometimes actively surface-feed. They are generally smaller, but it's fun just catching a couple of fish on the top once in a while. These fish will be sipping midges, but there have been times when a few active fish will key in on a sporadic Sulfur duo or two. A few of these Sulfurs can be found hatching even in the winter, but not often. Toward the end of this phase we often get a good hatch of Baetis, the little Olives. It is very exciting to run into this hatch in March. These little blue-winged mayflies appear to float in a line, and the trout may take up a feeding position and tip up time after time as the front end of a line of flies floats toward him. Usually a #20 or #22 dry with a brownish olive body, dark blue dun cut-wings, and a medium blue dun hackle does the trick. I like to tie this thorax-style with the hackle clipped on the bottom so the little fly floats flush on the surface. This mayfly dun floats a long way, its wings kept together as one. Sometimes this hatch will appear with a few Sulfur duns mixed in. Several years ago I ran into this phenomenon and was caught with only one suitable fly, a well-used Sulfur dun. I caught and released over twenty trout on a single fly. Time after time I straightened out the hook, but it did the job. The lesson here: Never be without a small box of dries, even on a winter fishing trip.

Phase two, or the early spring phase, begins with April Fools' Day. The principal difference here is that the water is warmer, making the fish more active. Best bets are the old standby cress bugs, shrimp, sculpin, and minnow patterns. Any day, one might intercept another Olive hatch, so be prepared. The early spring phase finds the grass growing and the trees thick with leaves. The biggest drawback of both the winter and the early spring phases is the lack of background cover. The fisherman is silhouetted against the sky and must take extra precautions to overcome this. After sunset is the best time for catching larger trout because fish that would spook during the day become more vulnerable at dusk. I have taken these on standard wet flies many times; surprisingly, the Pink Lady wet works well, as does the Gray Hackle Peacock and the Gray Hackle with a fur body. The larger fish usually succumb to a streamer fly. I'm always glad when this phase ends.

The spring to early summer phase, or phase three, from a dry-fly standpoint belongs to our favorite little mayfly, the Sulfur Dun, which has also been called the Little Yellow Drake or the Pale Evening Dun. Back in the 1930s, Charlie Fox and a few close fishing buddies started calling it the Sulfur, and this particular name has stuck. There are two species comprising the Sulfurs: the *Ephemerella dorothea* and the *Epeorus vitrea*. The *Epeorus* is a tad smaller. If my #16 imitation appears too large for the natural of the particular evening, I tie a #18 to the end of my 5X or 6X leader.

An important fly on the spring creeks of the West is the Pale Morning

Dun, another *Ephemerella (inermis)*; but the same Sulfur patterns can imitate the subimago (dun) and imago (spinner). These, as the names imply, are midmorning insects, which, when hatching in numbers, attract many fish. Once on Armstrong Spring Creek in Montana, Joe Brooks and I took turns working a group of surface-feeding trout. It wasn't until we switched to nymphs that our catch ratio picked up. This is a prime example of a fisherman being locked into a certain fishing pattern based on past experience. There are times when too much experience can be as harmful as not enough.

During late May and early June I sometimes run into another interesting midmorning occurrence: a concentrated hatch of Sulfur duns thick enough to bring a number of fish to the surface. Be cautioned that when it starts to happen you must get on it immediately because it may not last long. Although I saw this many times previous to the nineteen-sixties on the Letort, it has faded away due to a poisoning that devastated the insect population of the stream. As a result, the flies are so scarce even a good evening hatch no longer exists. Recently, I have again hit a morning hatch; Falling Spring usually has one that can be quite heavy for a short time, so when I have an opportunity to fish there in May or June I am disappointed if the duns do not show up. If you are concentrating on something else, the hatch can be over before you realize it.

Phase three, the hot-weather phase, begins with the first days of July and runs through mid-September. The Sulfurs are sporadic but can be found. We now run into the tiny *Tricorythodes*. I partially credit Ernie Schwiebert for the *Caenis* tag on the *Tricorythodes* mayfly. Back in the early nineteen-sixties, I was making the trip to Falling Spring every other Saturday morning to fish with my dear friend, Doctor Howard "Howdy" Hoffman. During July and August, we saw tremendous clouds of tiny mayfly spinners. Not being an entomologist, but still curious, I referred to my copy of Schwiebert's *Matching the Hatch*. The only tiny fly with two wings in that book was a *Caenis*. I started calling the little Trico by that name and it stuck; the name was further endorsed by Vince Marinaro, who was finally persuaded to come out of fishing retirement after I described this hatch. It was Vince who publicized the *Caenis* in an *Outdoor Life* story. After the story was published, the stream became so crowded on weekends that one needed a shoehorn to find a place to fish. After spending a few seasons on Falling Spring with only five or six fishermen on two miles of water, the crowds were a disappointment. But such is fly fishing.

The little Trico, as we call it now, is probably the last mayfly of importance on our chalk streams. This little two-winged fly emerges quickly from the water and in a few short hours becomes a spinner. Just last summer, while I camped along Montana's Missouri River, the Trico duns would begin to collect on the windows of the motor home at dusk and continued during the night. By daylight, the screens would be covered with the mayfly shucks, or shells, and the duns had become spinners. It was this all-night dun hatching that gave us the tremendous number of spinners the following morning. By 8 A.M. the tiny clouds of flies hovered ten to fifteen feet above the water. Lower and lower they descended until they landed. Hundreds of the dead or dying flies covered the water's surface. The trout rose to eat with a "slurp, slurp," sometimes swinging left, sometimes right, and other times plunging straight ahead. The fish's snout appeared above the water to inhale two or three flies. The fish would rest and repeat the process. The trick was to time the cast to coincide with the next rise. This can be fun fishing, but exasperating. Extreme accuracy and a drag-free float are the two most important things to aim for.

Although the Trico is not prevalent on the upper Letort, the lower Letort, from Carlisle downstream to its confluence with the warmwater Conodoguinet Creek, has excellent Trico fishing, with flies every bit as thick as on Falling Spring. This fishing has come about since a sewage treatment plant was shut down and a new one built on the warmwater stream. It has added four miles of good fishing to the Letort. Not too long ago, Joe Humphreys and I fished the spinner fall on the lower Letort and had two satisfying hours, releasing a large number of sassy trout up to a foot long. As the season progresses, the spinner fall comes later. By September, it may be eleven o'clock or noon before the flies touch down.

As in the best English tradition, the majority of anglers "fish the rise," casting only to feeding trout. At certain locations along the Letort, makeshift benches are found. Here, the angler rests to watch the water and locate rising trout. On other portions of the Letort the bench may be a fallen log, a railroad bridge, or a damp hummock of grass.

With the coming of the hot-weather phase, the terrestrials also find their "place in the sun." Along with the Tricos, the land-based insects are at their thickest and most active. The ants, of course, are on the water in varying numbers throughout the season, but now the grasshoppers are growing, as are the crickets. The little leafhoppers (Jassids) are happy to see the hot weather, and beetles of varying sizes and colors abound in the weeds. Jap beetles are clinging to the honeysuckle, wild roses, and jewel weed. Ants are dropping from bridges and tree limbs, and crickets and hoppers make directional mistakes on occasion and plop into the water.

Now the stream is at its fullest due to water displacement by increased weed growth. Great beds of elodea seem to be everywhere. Watercress and its relatives sprout eighteen inches above the water. The low banks become lush with grass shooting waist-high or higher. It is now that one must have a 9- or 10-foot fly rod to clear the weeds on a backcast. Unfortunately, I prefer short rods and didn't even realize I was using incorrect rod lengths for many years. The grass droops out over the water, creating dark tunnels that are the delight of big hungry trout. Here I watch for a rise tight against the grass, or spot a gentle wave motion from beneath the grass broadcasting the presence of a lurking trout. To cast an imitation of an ant, beetle, or Jassid that doesn't quite touch the grass so that the line of drift will sweep it past, is the greatest sport of all. The trout might be a youngster, or could be a brown in the 3- or 4-pound class. Bear in mind that we are essentially "fishing the rise." You could be fishing to a trout not in a rising but in a feeding position. The proportion of rises per cast will be greater when fishing to a feeding trout than when "fishing the water" with the smaller terrestrials.

In my opinion the finest terrestrial period is hopper time. The larger trout seem to anticipate the coming of the hopper, which begins with the tiny, immature bugs of early summer and ends with the full-grown hoppers of August. If a rise is spotted and an accurate cast is made, a hooked fish is inevitable. Casting to all inviting locations is even greater sport than this because it tests my ability to recognize the best holding water and pick out the hot spots such as the undercut banks, the overhanging brush or grass, or the patch of foam that collects in front of some obstruction. The unknown quantity holds the appeal. Is there a trout lying there? Is he hungry? Will he want what I offer him? How big is he? All these things run through my mind as I false-cast once or twice. The tiny cricket or hopper imitation lands just right and begins its float. As the fly swings in against the grass, it disappears with an audible *glurp*. I react, and a great brown begins a head-shaking dash for freedom. My tiny rod doubles as I do everything just right, and moments later the chunky brown is ready for the net. I ease two, three, or more pounds of trout onto the damp grass, admire the coloration, perhaps take a quick picture or two, and then remove the barbless fly and gently ease the trout back into the current. This, to me, is even more exciting than fishing the rise.

Chapter 5

Short FLY RODS

I thought of calling this chapter "My Love Affair with the Short Fly Rod" because that is exactly what it has been. It started many years ago with two articles by the great Lee Wulff, "The Light Touch," and "Throw It Out There." Numerous pictures of Lee with a hand-tailed salmon in one hand and a short bamboo rod in the other fired the imaginations of many fishermen, including this one. So, whether he enjoys the distinction or not, Lee has had more to do with short rod popularity than perhaps any other fisherman.

When these articles were published, there were only a few rod makers who advertised short fly rods: Orvis, with the Lee Wulff-sponsored 6-foot one-piece Superfine; and Paul Young, with his 6-foot 3-inch two-piece Midge. I now own two of the Orvis Superfines, but at that time the companies would not sell blanks, and I could not afford the completed rods. So I settled for 7-foot blanks from Orvis and Uslan instead. I regret not investing in the Paul Young Midge blanks, which were $15.00 for a two-piece set, including the ferrules, which were factory installed. What I wouldn't give for a couple of these little midge rods now – oh, hindsight!

I fished many years with the Orvis and Uslan 7-footers, and many trout bit the dust when I used them. Once, in a South Jersey stream, I landed eighty-two trout with the Uslan rod in less than five hours.

It wasn't until fiberglass, and a Teeny-Tiny 5½-foot rod from the Conolon Company, that I really went on a mini-rod binge. This rod opened up a whole new field of fly fishing for me; its initiation took place on the Coburn area of Penns Creek, a mighty stream by eastern standards. I was mapping the Millheim Quadrangle map for the U.S. Geological Survey at the time, and spent most weekday evenings tossing around a variety of tiny dries, big night streamers, and nymphs. I found in short order that I had to sharpen my timing and increase my casting speed. If I got sloppy with either, my backcast might drop too much and hit the water behind, or I might rap myself in the back of the head with the fly. Undaunted, I overcame most of these problems. I have found that if you are good enough to cast well with the shorter rods, you have no trouble at all handling the longer fly rods. That was one of the most enjoyable and rewarding fly-fishing summers I ever experienced, mainly because of this diminutive rod.

To me, a large part of fishing and hunting is aesthetic. A diminutive fly rod, neatly done, with a tiny grip to match and a plain reel seat is a joy to look at and carry, as is a short, slender, light-weight shotgun or rifle. As long as I am not chancing a crippling shot, I'll take the lightweight every time. The portability and beauty of the equipment are a great part of the game. Bear in mind that when I speak of fly fishing, I'm talking about average everyday trouting, with a little bluegill and bass fishing thrown in; steelhead and salt-water fishing are not included. So, for my fishing, diminutive rods are entirely adequate.

If you ask the average fisherman of today why he uses a long rod, you will get a broken-record recitation about holding more line off the water, mending the line better, and the ability to make longer casts. Long rod advocates preach that long rods are easier to fish with. If this is true, where's the challenge? Think about it. It is unfortunate that this preaching has had such an influence, because a lot of fishermen are missing some really fine, exciting, enjoyable fishing by not having a short rod or two in their rod batteries.

The introduction of graphite as a rod-building material has done much to increase the popularity of longer rods; a few years ago the long bamboo rod weighed five or six ounces. The same rod created from fiberglass weighed four ounces. Compare these to graphite, at three ounces, and boron, at slightly over three ounces. In prefiberglass days, the only way to go lighter was to go shorter. We found a whole new dimension of fly fishing in that not only were the rods lighter, but, because of the leverage factor, the fish, not the rod, was played. A fish seemed to pull harder and put up more of a fight because of the closer contact and the more direct energy transmission. Of course, the power of suggestion can do great things at times.

Erroneously, some fishermen feel short rods are more sporting, giving the fish a more even break; this is not so because of the leverage factor, and I find that fish can generally be played and landed much more quickly with the short outfit. In this day of catch-and-release, the more quickly a trout can be brought in and released, the better are the chances for his survival, assuming that the release is a clean one. Playing any trout until he is exhausted, then spending an hour holding him in the water, is not the sign of a true sportsman. With casts of reasonable distance, the faster casting tempo and subsequently faster line speed of short rods enable us to project the fly into a stiff breeze better than with a long-rod, using the same weight line. The long-rod advocate casts into a stiff breeze by using a heavy line, conflicting with the more delicate fishing I prefer.

Since I was born and raised in Carlisle, Pennsylvania, I grew up on the Letort. Oh how I love that stream! As fishing waters go, it is a small-to-medium stream and it is this type water I head for whenever I get the chance. I naturally like small waters best and it is on this type of water that my pet little rods get their best use.

After a few seasons with the Teeny-Tiny, I acquired a couple of one-piece fiberglass Grizzly rod blanks from a now-defunct Ohio firm. I made some one-piece rods, 5-foot 3-inches and 5-foot 6-inches long, which were suited for 4-weight lines, both double-tapered and weight-forward. I prefer floating lines.

While using these rods over a period of years, I have formed some short-rod likes and dislikes. The short fly rod should be flexible; the shaft should work crisply, almost down to the handle. A slow "wet noodle" type of action should be avoided, and the rod should be designed to work best with lighter fly lines. My pet rods handle the 4-weight lines best, but will

also handle a 3-weight. I do have a few rods that cast best with 5-weight lines, 4-weight being the second choice. If the rod casts comfortably at fifteen to thirty feet with a 4-weight, the chances are it will also cast from twenty to thirty-five feet with a 3-weight. So, if my selected rod for the day is to be used short range (up to thirty feet), I'll use a 4-weight line, but if I'm going to make a fair number of thirty-five-foot casts, I might opt for the 3-weight.

In the past I have used short rods that would not react properly unless matched with a 7- or 8-weight line. These were touted as 100-foot casting mini-rods, but if you're not happy unless you are casting 70 feet or more, go with a longer rod. Most casters who are not content unless their casts are long are the ones who damn the short rods. The "leetle ones" are designed for short-to-medium casts. These little rods shine in this range, and the effectiveness and pleasantness of the rod peaks there.

I like tiny rods to have small handles so I can use a much smaller grip without cramping my hand; a small grip on a larger rod causes discomfort quickly. I have tried a number of grip shapes but cannot find one more comfortable than the cigar shape, in various modifications. My preferred reel seat is cork, with a pair of sliding rings or a butt cap and one sliding ring. I design my reel seats to be just long enough to hold the reel. I use the Orvis Superfine grip style, the Hardy style, and a small-diameter cigar. Recently, I made a few short rods with a Paul Young-type handle, which is somewhat cylindrical, with a rounded front. I use both the thumb-on-top grip and the forefinger grip. By interchanging, fatigue and cramps are lessened. These are important factors when age and arthritis creep in.

The disadvantages of short rods are in keeping the line off the water, in mending the line effectively, and in the short casting distance. If these are important to you, forget the short rod. If I felt these factors were critical for catching or so fish, I wouldn't have caught twenty thousand or so fish on the real shorties, and another couple of thousand on my longer short rods (the 6- to 7-footers). Occasionally, even with a long rod, I drop my backcast and hang up in the grass behind me; but the advantages – portability, good looks, and general casting pleasantness – overcome the disadvantages. After a full day of casting and fishing the little rods I seldom feel any soreness in my forearm and wrist; I cannot make that statement when I have fished all day with a long rod. In addition, with a long rod I have to stay back farther from the edge when fishing undercut banks, and I lose visual contact with the fly.

Most fishing writers touting the ideal rod length write as if the fly rodder owns only one rod. Certainly, some fishers get their kicks out of seeing how little they can spend to come up with one usable outfit. But the average fisherman owns several rods and reels. Some time ago, *Fly Fisherman* magazine gathered statistics regarding rod ownership and found of those interviewed that 47% own 3.2 bamboo rods, 83% own 2.9 fiberglas rods, 63% own 2.5 graphite rods, and 19% own 3.3 homemade rods, presumably from rod kits. Possibly, some of these fishermen own two or three rods of the same length; the point is, although a single rod, say 8½ feet long, could suffice for everything from midges to bass bugs, why not vary rod lengths and usages? A short fly rod can be of more use on a large stream than can a long rod on a small brushy stream. Therefore, your rod battery should contain an 8½-footer, a 7-footer, and a 6-footer. These should suffice for average bass, panfish, and trout fishing on a variety of waters; naturally, the heavier, longer rods should be used on big water, where longer casts are the rule, and in bass bugging, where you cast fifty feet, retrieve ten feet, and pick up forty feet of line.

But I wouldn't use a short rod just to use a short rod. For a number of years I did use the short rods exclusively, even for some small-pond short-cast bass-bugging. Also during that time I caught hundreds of trout on nymphs and streamers, and even more on dries. Again, you might say I caught trout in spite of the handicaps, but these little rods really shine when used as dry-fly rods on relatively smooth, small waters where few conflicting currents are present.

On weed-filled streams like the Letort, I use the weed beds and high grass, which keep more line off of the water, as objects to cast over. Also, I generally present my fly (using a straight cast) as close to my quarry as possible so the trout will take it almost immediately. On occasion, when the trout are drifting back with the fly, waiting for it to drag, I put more slack in my cast. The Harvey leader formulas are great for this.

I usually use long leaders unless I'm fishing mountain brooks. Every-day leaders are 10 or 12 feet long and require drawing the line-leader connection through the tip guide many times. I want a connection that will flow back through the guides without the slightest hang-up, so I normally use the epoxy splice on every line, with a line leader butt of .017 inches of stiff mono. On occasion, when I will use a nail knot, I coat it with Pliobond for smoothness. I prefer the epoxy splice because I can extend the leader through the guides simply by false-casting. (Watch the contortions of the long-rod man when he tries to get his leader back out through the guides, particularly if he does not smooth up this connector knot.) The smooth epoxy splice is a godsend in the event the trout decides to run. This can be important whether you are using a long rod or a short rod.

I feel that too much emphasis is placed on perfection – seldom missing a rise or strike, never having the fly drag over a fish, and never making a mistake that might lose a fish. To be a perfect fly fisherman would be boring. The beginner should strive in the direction of perfection only because it will enable him or her to achieve some degree of casting finesse and fish-catching ability. I have had companions so upset over a missed fish that their days were ruined. If I do goof, my world doesn't crumble; I mentally reproach myself and straighten it out. Trying to outfish a friend is a certain way to ruin a friendship.

A number of seasons ago I had the pleasure of fishing with Mary and Joe Brooks on the Letort. I was using a 5-foot 4-inch fiberglass rod with a 4-weight-forward line. Joe and I were both catching fish on terrestrials. At dusk, as we sat and watched a number of rising fish, Joe turned to me and said "Ed, let me try that little rod of yours." The master only needed a second to get the tempo of the short stick before his first cast resulted in a rise and a hooked trout. After the release of the fish, a dandy, bright, 17-inch brown, Joe grinned at me and said, "Now I know why you like those little rods. That was fun." That, my friends, is the "short" of it. Fun is the name of this game.

Chapter 6

Fishing The
ITSY BITSIES

Charlie Fox calls it "The Art of Diminution," and Vince Marinaro called it "Pretty Fishing." In all the years I knew Vince, I feel sure that he favored "pretty fishing" over any other type. There comes a time in the life of every fly fisherman when using midges is a necessity if one wants to catch trout. At one time the term "midge" was used only to describe the tiny Diptera insects, and midge patterns were specifically designed to imitate them. Now we use the term loosely to describe not only the Diptera, but just about any relatively small fly, regardless of what it imitates. In this chapter, I deal with midges in the broad sense; the tiniest terrestrials are as important as aphids, small mayflies, and true midges.

A number of years ago, I wrote an article for *Field & Stream* magazine titled "The Minute Jassids." I wanted to call the article "A Little Larger than Nothing," after a comment I received from a passing fisherman. Showing him a #28 I was using, he snorted and said, "Hell, that ain't much bigger than nothing at all." The story dealt with the diminutive flies tied on #28 hooks and how to use them. Prior to my article, there was no published material dealing with flies tied on this smallest-eyed hook. At the time, these little hooks were gold-plated, but they are now available in the standard bronzed style.

The first flies I tried on these #28 hooks were tiny Fur Ants, Jassids, and Letort Beetles. The little beetle pattern was devised by Ernie Schweibert, who used an iridescent feather from the head of a male ring-necked pheasant. The feather was lacquered and trimmed to the desired size. I have seen many of these shiny beetles on the willow trees that abound by the waters I fish; we've always called them "willow beetles" for lack of a better descriptive name. Many times the trout keyed in on these beetles to the exclusion of the other available insects. When we watched the feeding fish and got the fly in the feeding lane without a drag, a rise was almost guaranteed. Hooking and landing the fish were more of a problem. During the course of one summer on the Letort and Breeches, when I was using the #28s (prior to my "miniature Jassid" article), I hooked and landed two brown trout slightly over 20 inches on #28 beetles. The legendary Lee Wulff took an Atlantic Salmon on a #28 fly not long ago, pointing out the fact that hooking, playing, and landing a big fish can be done on the smallest of flies.

Although an accomplished fisherman can use any fly tackle and fish midges successfully, the midge specialist usually has an outfit designed specifically for this diminutive game.

I feel that the line is more important than the rod, in the sense that midge fishing is best done with the lighter lines – preferably 2-, 3-, and 4-weights. Orvis has a graphite rod on the market that handles a 1-weight double-tapered line. Rods can range from between 5 and 6 feet to 9 feet long. I have caught many large and small trout while fishing with my little fiberglass and bamboo rods. The average fisherman is probably better equipped with rods over 6 feet long. Most rods built today and classed as midge rods are designed essentially to protect the lightest tippets on the strike and while playing a fish. Today's tippet material has a much higher pound-test rating than those used ten years ago, considering that not long after nylon came into use there was no 7X, and 6X was rated at one-half pound. I only dared use the 6X on very rare occasions, but remember landing at least one Letort fish over 19 inches long. Also, consider that this one-half pound rating was created before the knot was tied on the leader-tippet connector or on the clinch knot, near the fly. However, we landed fish in spite of these handicaps. A few expert fly fishers swore by the long stiff rods for midges, reasoning that guide friction was less, therefore less pressure was placed on the leader. The only fallacy with this is that many fish are broken off on the strike, even with the more flexible-tipped rods. Given two rods of equal length, though, one could strike a little bit harder with the softer-tipped rod than with a stiff tip.

One way to minimize breaking off on the strike is simply to raise your rod hand without rearing back. This increases the pressure on the tiny hook by keeping more line off the water. Bear in mind it takes very little pressure to embed the little hooks, #20 to #28, assuming that the hook points are fairly sharp. Another striking method used by a few good midgers who haven't quite controlled their striking impulses, is to strike without holding the line in your other hand. Assuming you have some slack line between the reel and the butt or stripping guide, raise the rod with a little slack line pulled forward toward the butt guide. This creates a cushion for the fly-end of the tackle. No matter which method you end up using, practice is the key, as in all areas of fly fishing. I suggest that anyone desiring to become an accomplished midge fisherman should forsake the other flies and spend a few weeks fishing only midges. The more time you spend at this game, the more competent you should become. Call this "Shenk's Law" if you will. As I mentioned earlier in this chapter, I spent one entire summer fishing almost exclusively with #28s. By the time that summer was over I rarely broke off a fish except of course those that ran into weeds or snags. I seldom made the mistake of striking too hard; I knew what the terminal tackle could take and exploited the tolerances.

Now with a rod between 6 and 9 feet long, casting a 1-, 2-, or 3-weight line, we need the reel. The smaller single-action reels with light drag get my nod every time. Some writers prefer the reels with slightly larger diameters so the line does not come off the reel in tiny coils, but for big-water streams, a reel the size of the Orvis CFO III, the Hardy Feather-weight, or similar-size reels are better. There are a plethora of lightweight fly reels on the market today; one can find a reel to fit nearly any budget, with some costing well over a hundred dollars. Bear in mind that the higher-priced reels generally have a smoother drag system, which is an essential part of the fly-fishing game and a critical part of midge fishing. I prefer to play most fish from the reel—a good habit to adopt for the least

break-offs when the drag is the smoothest. An inexpensive reel can some-times be hand-tuned to create a very light, smooth drag. If it cannot be tuned correctly, it should be used for heavier fishing.

Lines should be light and should cast well on your rod. Heavy lines create more water resistance than do light ones, and can actually resist to the point of breaking even a light tippet, even with the most careful han-dling. In addition, a clean, well-lubricated line creates less friction on the rod guides and will therefore slightly increase your odds.

Leaders with long tippets always get the nod. Long tippets have more stretch than do short ones, thereby cushioning the strike better. A longer tippet will also allow the fly more natural freedom, which is important. I like them between 24 and 30 inches long. When they shorten to 21 inches or so, I replace them with a longer one. We think of 6X, 7X, and 8X as the midge tippets. It is my theory that if a 6X is working, why switch to a 7X? The same theory applies to a 7X versus an 8X. There have been times when an 8X has been necessary, but fortunately this is rare. I usually use a 6X on flies to #22, and a 7X for #24s and #28s. I think that when the fish are focused in on such tiny flies a slightly larger leader is out of place, as is a tiny fly with a big clinch knot. A final advantage of the lighter leaders is flexibility.

Not long ago I read an article where the author stated that when he uses the smallest flies he does not fish the water but casts only to feeding fish. I cannot imagine fishing the tiniest midges unless a fish is visible; it doesn't take much imagination to realize that unless a tiny fly is very close to a fish, it will simply go unnoticed. So we have midge terrestrials, little ants, beetles, leafhoppers (Jassids), and aphids. The little aphids look like bits of pale blue lint floating around. I like to tie them with a pale blue or cream-colored body, no tail, and the smallest pale blue or cream hackle, using about two turns. This tiny fly has often fooled a number of steadily rising fish when they would barely look at any other pattern.

Another excellent dry pattern is the No Name, which I tie in #20 to a #28. This is a good general-purpose midge pattern, one of the best I have tried. It is simply a miniature gray-hackle, gray-body fly. I tie mine with medium gray muskrat fur dubbing for the body and a tiny grizzly hackle. I once simply called this the Grizzly Midge, but "No Name" came about in an unusual way. The late Norm Lightner of Carlisle liked to fish Big Spring Creek at Newville for the free-rising native brookies that were numerous in the early 1960s. One of his favorite flies was a #20 Grizzly Midge. On one occasion Vince Marinaro was watching Norm take a number of brookies, when he finally eased over and asked, "What are you getting them on?" When Norm showed Vince the little fly, Vince snorted and replied, "There ain't such a fly. It doesn't imitate anything I ever saw. It doesn't have a name." That is how the No Name came about.

I recall many times when the little No Name pattern outdid all others on the Allenberry section of the Yellow Breeches. I even landed some fish close to 20 inches long on a #20 No Name in the dark. The trick was to fish a tight line, rod tip high, and use a slow, skimming retrieve. The tiny skimming fly gave off a little luminescent wake for any nearby fish to see.

A bright, perfect October day was the setting for another very memorable midging episode. Proceeding slowly through the shallow water near the Allenberry Pavilion, I had on a tapered leader ending in a long 6X tippet. Numerous fish were in feeding position, sipping tiny insects as they drifted by. I would pick out a trout and place a cast nearby, and almost every trout inhaled the tiny No Names. As I released each fish, I often bent or broke the fragile hooks. I quickly used up my meager supply of No Names and tried tiny ants and other midges, to no avail. I finally found a perfect little #22 Adams with tiny matched grizzly-hackle-tip wings. I knotted it on and tried it over a number of trout with no takers. They would swing over, closely inspect it, and turn back to their feeding positions. After pondering this awhile, I tearfully pulled the tiny wings from the fly. The first cast resulted in a take, and many more fish were caught before the fly was worn out. A good friend, Bill Braught, who was fishing nearby, commented, "Ed, I watched the fisherman behind you as you started to catch trout after trout. He literally stood there with his mouth wide open as he watched you for about twenty minutes. Finally, he just said 'I don't believe it,' and left the stream." Who says wings are always necessary?

Another group of important midge patterns are the tiny fur nymphs tied on #18 and smaller hooks. I like to weight these slightly so they penetrate the surface film quickly. The best colors are green, brown, tan, and black, ribbed with gold wire. One of these, a little one made from brown weasel fur with the guard hairs left in, and ribbed with gold wire, became known as the Shenk Special. These can readily imitate the true midge pupae as well as various other morsels. Another pattern is tied with bright orange fur and very slender, like a tiny worm; I also like to rib this one with gold wire. Wire adds segmentation to the bodies, as well as a bit of sparkle. I put dark fur, black ostrich herl, or peacock herl at the head end of some of these, imitating the midge pupae. These add variety, but only rarely do they actually decide the difference between a fair day and super day of fishing.

During September 1987, I ran into tremendous midge activity on the Missouri River. Gary LaFontaine has described this river as a giant spring creek, and I agree. It is hard to believe fish could become so selective, but that is exactly what happened here; the super *Tricorythodes* spinner fall was all but ignored while the fish fed incessantly. On occasion, I fooled a trout on a #24 Trico spinner, but my average was down. A close inspection of the first fish caught, a 20-inch rainbow, revealed its mouth and throat crammed full of rather large, bright green Diptera pupae. I tied an imitation on #18 hooks and several on #16. I allowed more of the bend of the hook to show on the #16s, but the biggest problem was with presenting the fly to the fish, or getting them to see it. The fish were cruisers, although they stayed in a bathtub-size piece of water. They would swing left, take some pupae, immediately surge forward, take some more, then turn around and take a few on the way downstream. It was maddening; they just wouldn't hold still. Once the imitation was seen, there was generally no refusal, but getting them to see it was difficult. Some of the fish popped the tippet on their first run, which was quite a thrill. But even on 6X I was able to hold a number of fish. This was a case where even the 5X tippet showed a drop in number of takers. I could see the fly hit the water and watch a fish surge for it and swerve away at the last minute, but when I dropped down to 6X the refusals diminished. Occasionally, a fish took an adult midge decidedly smaller than the pupae. I tied imitations on a #22 hook and succeeded in landing a couple of super browns and rainbows close to 20 inches long, which was a feat because the surging fish were powerful. On numerous occasions, though, one was lost when close to being landed. I play my fish hard so they won't have much energy to expend during the landing and release. But the ones that got off were not really missed because they were slated for release anyway. The midges have become my western-river standbys.

Let's take these next few paragraphs and do some midge fishing on the Yellow Breeches. The late September day is bright, the water is clear, and I can see a number of sipping rises upstream. I'm using a light 6½-foot graphite rod, matching 3-weight floating line, and a 12-foot leader ending in a 24-inch section of good 6X (.005 inch) leader material. I tie on a #22 No Name, add a little mucilin paste to the fly, and run the leader through mucilin-coated fingers. I do this on all but the last foot or so of the 6X tippet to allow my leader to float and make my pickup much easier. I'm wearing green non-reflective clothing and have removed my watch. I do not want any flash of clothing to alert the cautiously feeding trout. I watch the first fish for a minute or two, trying to determine whether he is actually surface-feeding or sipping in the film. This one, a brown approximately 12 inches long, is doing both surface-feeding and taking an underwater morsel once in a while. I'm to the rear-right of this fish, so I make my cast about a foot upstream and ever so slightly to the right. I might get away with a cast directly over the fish, but the chance of the fish bumping the leader on the rise dictates my pitch. The tiny fly alights gently, just where I want it to, drifting down until it is quietly sucked in by the unsuspecting trout. A second's hesitation and a slight raising of the rod is all it takes. I get a clean hookup, gently play the fish from the reel, and release it by holding the fly between my thumb and forefinger and giving it a little twist.

As I proceed upstream, I repeat the procedure on a few more browns, each one completely fooled by the tiny grizzly-hackled fly. I watch another fish in tight to the right-hand bank as it swings left each time to take a natural. I get a few decent casts slightly to the left, but the fly is inspected and refused each time. "Here's a selective one," I grumble. I get close to the water's surface and see a parade of tiny ants drifting downstream. Knotting on a tiny #26 Cinnamon Ant, I make a pitch and get an immediate response. Unfortunately, I strike too hard and not only "tick" the fish but also scare it; he won't be back for a while. My approach to the next couple fish is off, and I scare them before I even get a good cast to them.

Ahead I see the flash of a nice fish as it takes something about a foot under the surface. With my Polaroid glasses I watch the fish, about 17 inches long, as it drifts left, then right. I can see its mouth open and close each time some little morsel is taken. I back off a little on this one so I don't give myself away before I get a good cast to it. I snip the tiny ant from the tippet and pick out one of the little fur midges. This one is a medium brown with the tiny body segmented with gold wire. I check the hook to make sure the barb is pinched down, and, at the same time, I offset the hook bend slightly. This offset gives slightly better hooking than does a straight bend.

Quietly, I ease into the water below the fish, reach down, and soak the fly by pinching it like a tiny sponge underwater. As an afterthought, I reach the bank and take a tiny pinch of mud, rubbing it over the tippet only. I want this part of the leader to sink this time. My cast is upstream from the trout and passes slightly to the left. I watch the fish and see it glide slightly to the left and mouth something; instantly I react, and the fish is on. It jumps at the sting of the hook and then heads up and across the stream. As the line screeches from the reel, I ease the tension by lowering my rod tip. This reduces the friction of the line on the rod guides, lessening the chances of the fish breaking off. (This is an important action and well worth practicing.)

The heavy brown finally comes closer and shortly I am admiring a yellow-bellied red-spotted holdover fish, exactly 15 inches long. Since I prefer to play my fish as hard as the tackle will permit, the brown is not half dead when I release it. Nothing makes less sense to me than gently worrying a nice fish to total exhaustion, and then spending another hour attempting to revive it; many times these fish cannot be revived. I have seen this type of release and then watched as the apparently revived fish later rolled over and died. Know what your tackle will do, and then do it.

The sun is descending as I release the brown—a good fish with which to conclude a perfect fall afternoon of fishing. I place the little midge nymph in the hookkeeper just above the rod handle, nod to the stream, and head toward the van.

Chapter 7

SULFURS

Shadows lengthened as the late afternoon sun slanted westward. I sat impatiently (and damply) on a rotting log, watching the currents of the fabled Letort for any sign of surface activity. It was mid-May, and any minute I expected to see a number of pale yellow mayflies struggling along the water's surface prior to lifting off and heading for the protection of nearby trees.

Charlie Fox says he gave the name *Sulfur* to this beautiful mayfly back in the 1930s, when I was just starting my fly-fishing career. (I might mention in passing that the words *sulfur* and *sulphur* are interchangeable according to the dictionary, and both mean a pale orange-yellow color.) Sulfur is usually a name given to the *Ephemerella dorothea* mayfly. In some areas they are called "Dorotheas," but I like the name given them by Charlie Fox. In Ernest Schwiebert's book *Matching the Hatch* he calls the pale little *Epeorus vitrea* a Sulfur.

As the season goes forward, the Sulfur dun is thought to become progressively smaller, which would mean that by late summer the Sulfur would be equivalent in size to a #22. Such is not the case. On occasion, the

Sulfurs hatch slightly smaller than the normal size of a #16. These smaller ones are about the size of a #18, and I have a hunch these are the *vitreas* instead of the *dorotheas*. If your normal #16 appears too large and the fish are refusing it, dig out the appropriate #18 dun or spinner. The next night the flies will probably be best imitated by the larger pattern again.

My observations regarding the Sulfur come mainly from experiences on local streams, including the Letort, Yellow Breeches, Big Spring, Green Spring, and Falling Spring, but the methods and patterns work wherever the Sulfur is found. I have also used all my Sulfur patterns successfully in Montana and Wyoming waters. If the dun is pale yellow and about the size of a #16, it doesn't matter which species it is or where it is found.

With the exception of the Yellow Breeches, local streams do not have the true cycle of the season mayfly hatches. The Letort, for instance, has a sporadic Blue-winged Olive hatch, and the lower section of river has a good Trico spinner fall, but the Sulfur is the most important hatch during May and June. Falling Spring, famous for its Trico spinner fall during summer and autumn, also has a terrific Sulfur hatch during midseason. Peak Sulfur emergence usually occurs from mid-May until mid-June. However, I have seen sporadic Sulfur activity every month on the Letort. In late February 1984, I was trying to entice a few fish on sculpin patterns when I began to notice a number of rising trout in one shallow section of the stream. A few Sulfur duns were winging skyward but, due to the chill, the flies drifted far before becoming airborne, and the trout were taking them. When I fish early in the season, I am seldom up to full pattern strength, and this February day was no exception. A desperate search through a number of fly boxes finally turned up one lonely, well-used Sulfur pattern tied on a light-wire Captain Hamilton hook. Using that single fly, I shortly landed and released over twenty browns, the longest fish over 16 inches. At one point I made ten casts and hooked and landed ten trout – what a refreshing little episode! The moral – carry a few Sulfur patterns at all times because you may encounter dun activity in any season.

The best Sulfur fishing usually occurs after sunset. All day, the duns hatch sporadically; as the sun drops lower the duns generally increase in number until the fish start rising to them. Some authors believe the dun is not readily taken and does not create the rising response that the spinner

does; however, I have often seen the duns avidly sucked in by eager trout. It is also believed Sulfur duns become airborne very quickly, hence the trout's reluctance to take them. Although there are evenings when this happens, usually hot nights with low humidity, on cool evenings the duns often drift for dozens of feet before becoming airborne, and I have even watched fortunate individual flies drift for several hundred feet before being sucked in or becoming airborne. As in most of fishing, there are always exceptions to the rules.

There are several important aspects of the Sulfur during the subimago (dun) stage. On any stream, the evening hatch of duns may be clustered — hot and heavy in one area, and sparse to nonexistent in another section of the same stream. On one particularly favorite stretch of water, I once had a great final hour of daylight fishing. Two evenings later the same pools were devoid of flies, while a few hundred yards upstream and downstream there were great things going on. This is common on the streams I fish regularly. Some British fly-fishing journals mention that when a heavy mist hangs on the water, the rise is nonexistent. This may be valid ninety percent of the time, but I have had exciting fishing to rising trout in heavy mists. Years ago there was a morning hatch of short duration on the Letort, and if I hit it right, I could fool a number of fish before the duns diminished. Recently, this phenomenon has reappeared on the Letort.

For a number of years following a stream poisoning on the Letort in the early 1960s, even the evening dun and spinner activity was nonexistent, except for the Right Branch, what we call Trego's Meadow. This branch provided terrific fishing even though the majority of Sulfur fishermen stayed home. It was from this branch that the stream insects repopulated the entire stream. Although the poisoning nearly wiped out the stream insects, minnows, cress bugs, shrimp, crayfish, and mayflies, it did not appear to affect the trout; however, bottom-feeding suckers were hit hard. I could not find a single cress bug from Bonny Brook to Carlisle. The good news is that the morning hatch of Sulfur duns is once more on the upswing, and its appearance is now a possibility on any May or June day.

The Sulfur spinners seem to prefer the aerated water of riffle and gravel beds and are mostly found clustered here. Sadly, there are sometimes tremendous spinner clusters over macadam roads, where the eggs, consisting of a few to hundreds of flies, are wasted. The spinners seldom hit the water before dusk, and in July and August an occasional cloud of spinners gathers long after dark, when most fishermen have left the stream. If I can manage to get a spinner tied on, and it is legal to fish after dark in the area, I have had satisfying action when trout are taking them. After more than fifty years of intensive trouting, I can now walk away from rising fish, particularly after I have already caught a few. I have never bothered to capture these late-season spinners for close study, but they appear to be the same size and color as the flies of May and June. A #16 imitation generally fills the bill.

Back in my earlier days on the Letort, the common pattern was a Pale Cahill, #14 or #16, tied onto a tapered leader ending in a 3X tippet. This was in the days of Spanish or Japanese gut leaders; I was in my midteens when nylon finally came along. Today, we are all a little more sophisti-cated, as are the trout; although I can still catch a brown or two on the Pale Cahill, it has been ages since I fooled a Sulfur-eater on a 3X leader. I prefer a 5X, because a #16 dry and a 5X seem to go together like bacon and eggs. Occasionally, a long, flexible 4X tippet has fooled fish, but I find fewer refusals using a 5X. 6X tippets often result in twisting, unless the fly is sparsely tied. My recommended tippet size is 5X, around two feet long. If the tippet twists, I shorten it by an inch or two and try again. My leaders start with a butt section seldom greater than .017 inches, and taper to the desired tippet diameter.

Lines should match the rod, of course, but this is a chance to use the light lines with matching rods. Whichever rod I am using is complimented with a 3- or 4-weight line. Whether the line is double-tapered or weight-forward is purely academic. Most casts are short, and a weight-forward doesn't get to do its job until more than thirty feet of it extends past the rod tip. I recommend a light-colored or fluorescent line because it enables one to judge the position of the fly in the fading light.

Rods are a subject of constant controversy. Many writers recommend long rods and others suggest short ones. Bear in mind that casts are usu-ally short, and since you are pinpointing casts to rising trout, you'll usually cast the fly for minimal drift before it reaches the fish. The Sulfur has long been my favorite mayfly hatch, and I prefer to use my battery of diminu-tive bamboo rods, which range from 4-feet 8-inches to 6-feet 6-inches in length. Some of these rods are used only one or two evenings a season; others, like my Thomas & Thomas 6-foot 1-piece Individualist, and my Orvis 6-foot Superfine, see more service. I use the shorter graphites and, on occasion, a little fiberglass rod, but this dry-fly fun game is made for the little bamboos.

Fishing the Sulfur spinner is no different mechanically than fishing the dun imitation. However, the spinner is the last phase on the water, often not seen until darkness sets in. I try to position myself to look into the fading light. This will add at least thirty minutes to my fishing time. Before it gets too dark to do so, I remove the Sulfur dun from my leader and tie on one of my favorite spinner patterns, waterproofed and ready to go. Usually, the fish key in on the spent-wing spinners at this stage of the game. When the spinners first begin to hit the water, the trout are still sucking in the moving insects with their dying kicks and flutters; the dun pattern can be as effective as the spinner at this point. A little twitch of the rod tip will sometimes put an extra "something" into the drift, so don't be afraid to experiment. Experience trains the caster to make his pitch at the right distance to cover a particular rise; even if I cannot see the fly, I know about where it should be. Watching for a rise and striking accordingly, I sometimes see the little wink of light where the fly hits the water, about a foot or so upstream from the rise, and an inch or so off to the side. Often, the fish are seeing better toward the west, so, if possible, I cast to the side favoring the brightness.

There are many facets to the fishing game. For instance, I prefer to be positioned slightly off to one side and below my rising fish. In this way I cast up and across stream to cover them. However, circumstances can be such that I must be positioned directly downstream from the rises. Many times I have made the mistake of casting directly over the fish and its nose nudges the tippet as it attempts to inhale the fly. This usually results in a missed fish. I try to cast the fly slightly to one side or the other so that the trout has to turn its head to suck in the imitation. This is an extremely important tactic. One time in particular, when the light was quickly fading, I decided that the current riser would be my last for the evening. I saw the rise, hit it precisely with a cast about six inches upstream from the trout's nose, and the fish took the fly. I struck and never touched it. The fish took a few more naturals, I repeated the cast, drift, rise, and missed three more times. I was dumbfounded. It finally dawned on me that the fish was bumping the tippet with its nose and pushing the fly out of the way. My next cast was slightly to the right – the brightly lit side. The rise came as usual, I set the hook, and nothing happened. The little bamboo rod bent dangerously and the fly was into something solid. "Damn," I muttered, "after all that, and I mess up by hooking a log." After a few moments the "log" started to move and, after a spirited series of runs, swirls, and splashes, I put my hand under the belly of a male brown nearly two feet long, my best catch with a Sulfur. Gently I released the old resident and watched him disappear into the river.

About fifty years ago, the Sulfur was "on" and my dad and I were fishing the Quarry Meadow of the Letort along with a number of other anglers. I was doing things right that evening, and had landed four nice browns.

Perhaps I was fishing dumb fish, because no one else was doing well. A slight gentleman with horn-rimmed glasses and a flat-woven creel on his side walked up and congratulated me on my success, saying, "You are really doing a good job on these Letort trout, son." Of course everyone likes a pat on the back, but how many can claim receiving that pat from Ray Bergman?

At times, trout feed selectively on the emerging nymph. The trout appear to be rising regularly, yet they ignore a well-presented dry fly. There may be imperceptible drag, but in many instances it is because the trout have really keyed in on the emerger. In this situation, my answer is to tie on an emerger pattern or a cream-colored wet fly that will work just under the surface. Ernie Schwiebert has written of using a Little Marryat wet fly very similar to the Light Cahill, except that the wing is a pale gray duck quill instead of lemon wood duck. I cast down and across to the false-risers so that the fly swings just in front of the fish. Keep the rod tip high to cushion the shock of a heavy strike. A big trout on a tight line, especially if the rod is not used to cushion the first shock, may very well break off.

A few seasons back I did a piece for *Fly Fisherman* magazine called "Sulfurs – Variations on a Theme." In the article, I mentioned a large variety of patterns I have found successful for both dun, spinner, and nymph. All are useful, and the variety is considerable. A principal reason for variety in catch-and-release water is due to fishing pressure, which is much greater than on the average open-water stream. Fly fishing for trout in open water is generally easier than in water where all or most fish are returned. Although open water has fewer remaining trout, those holdovers have been bombed with a variety of baits, lures, and spinners, and any well-presented Sulfur dun pattern should do the trick.

The old adage "variety is the spice of life" holds true for fly imitations, especially the popular ones, such as the Sulfur, particularly in catch-and-release areas. During my teenage years there were only a few Sulfur imitations in everyday use. A buff-colored Light Cahill was *the* fly, with its pale cream fox-fur body and lemon wood-duck wings. I had trouble tying wings then, so I fished with the wingless variety more often. A decent-size trout was frying-pan fodder in those days, and the little fish continued to get caught each night during the peak of the hatch. On catch-and-release waters, where many of us released our catch, it was possible to fool the same big trout three or four times over a period of weeks. Once a good fish is located, you can bet he'll stay in the same spot until he is scared away or killed.

Early in the Sulfur hatch one season, I was working my way upstream on my favorite stretch of the Letort. Numerous rises were observed, and I tried to cover as many of them as I could. Most good floats brought a complete rise. Using the buff-colored hackle pattern, I caught and released a number of brightly colored browns, and every so often a native brookie even more beautiful than the browns. I knelt to tie a fresh fly to my 5X tippet, and as I did, I continued to watch upstream out of the corner of my eye for additional rising trout. Particularly intriguing was a heavy rise in the slack water just upstream from a partially submerged log. The duns would drift downstream into the slack, pause momentarily, and then disappear in a bulge of water. "Good fish," I thought, as I hurriedly dressed the fly and leader with a thin film of mucilin dressing. In this situation, the trick is to cast over the obstruction with just enough leader to permit the fly to land momentarily in the little backwater. My artificial danced in the slack water and disappeared just like the naturals. I set the hook, then moved quickly upstream to clear my leader of the log; then, a steady pull to the side threw the brown off balance enough for me to force it from its protective cover. I soon netted a hefty brown slightly longer than 20 inches. A quick twist of the barbless hook and the fish swam free.

A few evenings later I was fishing the same beat, catching some of the same fish, when the big brown was back. Always interested in the unexpected, I hit the spot with the same pattern I used before. There was a bulge of water under the fly but it remained floating as I inched it back over the log without hanging up. I waited a few minutes until the trout started taking naturals again, then I tied on a George Harvey Sulfur, which had cream hackle-tip wings with one orange hackle for color. It rode the slack just right and disappeared in the rise of a completely fooled trout. Once again we fought the same battle, and once again I released the same big male brown.

It was another week before I got back to the stream, and the Sulfur duns were coming off very well. I was looking forward to another try at the big brown. This time I tied on a third dun imitation, a cut-wing thorax tie that, at least from a distance, looked identical to the naturals on the water.

I waited, but no rise came to the dancing duns drifting into the slack water. Did someone kill the big one? I wondered. In the gathering dusk I could see a ball of spinners dancing their last farewells. Quickly I snipped the good-looking dun from my tippet and knotted on an orange-bodied poly-wing spinner while it was still light enough to see. (On a good evening, the last fly of the day may account for a half-dozen fish or so.) I imagined a little disturbance ahead of the log. "Could it be?" I asked myself. I could feel when the cast was lengthened enough and made my pitch; for what seemed like hours the fly hung in the backwater before it disappeared. I felt a heavy surge as I set the hook, and seconds later I was without a fly. The old boy had learned a trick or two. Several mornings later I caught the same brown on a large floating ant. The little poly-wing was still sticking in the roof of the trout's mouth. I didn't bother that fish again and hope he lived out his days without another person trying to stab him with a hook.

Each spring I find myself looking forward to surface trout fishing, and for me that begins with the little *Ephemerella*, the Sulfur.

Chapter 8

The Skater
WALTZ

Bluebird days in midsummer are usually the bane of the fly fisher. We can look for a shaded portion of stream and fish terrestrials such as ants, hoppers, and crickets, or we can try another hot-weather game that sometimes eclipses the terrestrial fishing – fishing the Skater Spiders.

Edward Ringwood Hewitt is credited with the origination of the Skater Spider. He called his fly the Neversink Skater and his fishing of it "butterfly fishing." Presumably, his original intent was to suggest a butterfly as it flitted over the water's surface. Hewitt's original spider was tied to a #16 hook, with rooster-spade hackles that sometimes exceeded two inches in diameter. He used this fly as a trout locator, but it was a poor hooking pattern because of the relationship between the small hook size and the stiffness and diameter of the hackle. The stiff hackles, in a sense, acted as a weed guard.

When I began fishing skaters, I too found them to be poor hookers, but the excitement of moving larger fish on bright, hot afternoons in crystal clear water far outweighed the poor hooking percentages. Much later, I found that a delayed strike helped increase the number of hooked fish per strike. I remembered the locations of the trout I attracted and missed, and later caught many of these fish on other flies, such as the Hard-bodied Ant or the tiny white marabou.

For years I classified the big skaters as attractor patterns even though I would occasionally hook a trout while using one. When I went to a larger hook with a slightly smaller-diameter hackle, my hooking percentages improved. From the late 1930s to the mid-1950s, I usually carried a few of these flies in my box, using them on special occasions when the weather dictated it. Then, two enterprising fly fishermen, Norm Lightner and Albert "Tommy" Thomas, both from Carlisle, Pennsylvania, began using silver-dollar-size skaters during their yearly pilgrimages to the streams of Wyoming's Yellowstone Park and southwestern Montana. The big trout devoured their skaters, and each man put at least one trout on the "Wall of Fame" in Dan Bailey's shop in Livingston. (Fish for this wall must weigh over 4 pounds to qualify).

During this period, the late Joe Brooks regularly met Norm and Tommy on various streams, and after seeing the success of the big flies he became excited about the patterns. Joe subsequently wrote an article titled "The Skater's Waltz" for a national outdoor magazine and devoted several paragraphs in his book *Trout Fishing* and in later editions of *The Complete Book of Fly Fishing* to the patterns. Chapter 7 of Charlie Fox's book *This Wonderful World of Trout* is devoted to skaters. Some of my early fishing memories are of Charlie Fox skimming the Neversink Skaters across the Letort; the buff-colored Honey Skater is still his favorite. Norm supplied Joe Brooks with skater flies and also tied for Ed Koch's fly shop, where I worked for a time. With Norm's passing, the job of tying these skaters was left to me. Over the years, I supplied Joe with many dozen flies in various sizes and patterns. The most popular were the #8, #10, and the #12, not the usual #16. Apparently, in his experiences as well as mine, the larger sizes were better hookers.

Once, Joe called and ordered a large number of big spiders as a gift for his dear friend Jose "Bebe" Anchorena of Argentina. Apparently, he found these flies to be deadly on the *muy grande trucha* (great trout) found in the rivers of the Argentine Andes. I picked and repicked the big rooster necks, whose hackles were used for the outsized skaters, but found it impossible to get hackles with an extra-wide spread. Consequently, my amigo from Argentina has had to be content with skaters of a smaller diameter. Perhaps I will someday have the opportunity to spend some time fishing the famous waters of western Argentina with my friend Bebe.

I have fished many western rivers since the mid-1960s, especially those within a 150-mile radius of West Yellowstone. I have enjoyed bright cloudless afternoons when it was difficult to get fish to come to a regular dry unless I fished the shaded edges, but a Skater Spider moved fish in these waters. Many times on the Madison, where fish were jumping for dragonflies and other hovering insects, a dancing skater fished up and across stream, or down and across stream and skated back, was the only way to go.

I also remember fishing skaters in a long, deep pool on the Big Hole below Melrose as the sun dropped behind the hills and the wind died to a gentle whisper. I was casting thirty to forty feet of line and leader, fishing across the pool and slightly downstream. I would make a few casts and then ease a step or two downstream, repeating the cast after planting my feet. I don't like to cast and walk or wade at the same time. Once the fly is on the water, I don't move my feet until the cast is completed and I'm ready to cast again. The skater reminded me of a long-legged cranefly as I retrieved it in a steady manner, making it wiggle, dance, and bounce to give it a lifelike look.

After catching a couple of 2-pound-class fish on one skater, I tied on a fresh one that rode "tippy toe" on the placid water. I shot the fly across so it would light just ahead of an enticing overhanging bank. I held my breath as something appeared to stalk the fly. At first I thought it was a passing beaver, but the wake continued toward the fly. I stopped my retrieval by lowering the rod, and waited for the fish to close in, then I started the retrieve again.

As far as spider rises go, the take was a gentle one but was accompanied by a tremendous snout breaking the surface with a sound like a cow pulling her feet out of the mud. I reared back and was fast to a truly great Big Hole brown. In seconds I was staring at a rapidly emptying reel spool. As the fish's run continued, the pressure on the line and leader increased and it panicked. One tremendous jump concluded the action. I still had the bedraggled fly, but the hook was nearly straightened. My angling companion heard the fish jump nearly 500 yards upstream. I wish I could say that I returned and caught the old leviathan, but it didn't happen. I never saw that fish again except in my dreams.

The true skater is nothing more than a hook, thread, and hackles tied in a particular way. The only differences between patterns are the sizes and hackle color, so I'll list several patterns in order of preference by Joe, Norm, Tommy, and myself. They are: 1) The Adams Hackle (brown and grizzly mixed); 2) The all-black (this is the Argentina favorite); 3) The Buffalo (brown and black mixed); 4) The Badger (cream or white with a black center); 5) The Furnace; and 6) The Light Ginger. As I mentioned previously, the Honey Skater is a favorite of Charlie Fox.

Tying these flies is not really complicated, just different. Choose your hackle from the side of a big rooster's neck. I'm continually on the lookout for necks capable of producing suitable spiders, and they are difficult to find because the emphasis is on breeding roosters for necks with long slender feathers. When I find one with very long fibers and minimal webbing I jump for joy and think of my friend Bebe Anchorena.

To help yourself understand how to tie a spider, cup your hands slightly and place them with the palms together and fingertips touching. This is exactly what I try to do with the hackle: tie them so the tips come together. The larger hooks (#8 and #10) will take four or five hackles, with the three rear ones cupped forward and the front ones cupped from the rear so the tips touch somewhat. Smaller hooks will require four feathers (two and two). If I have fairly long hackle, I may use two rear hackles and one front hackle. On the smallest flies I use two feathers, one forward and one to the rear. The feather is wound forward and the next feather is woven into the first feather as *it* is wound forward. Continue this on the third feather if this is a larger fly. When this is complete, and before the tips are trimmed, compress the hackle winds tightly toward the bend of the hook. I usually do this with my right thumb and forefinger, pushing toward the rear of the hook. When these are compacted, the front feathers are tied in and wound the same way. To achieve the cupping position, remember that the rear hackles will have their shiny sides to the rear and the front ones will have the shiny sides forward. Once the fly is finished, I put "goop," or flexament, on the hackles and work them together. This add stiffness to the fly, which is necessary if the fly is to ride on the tips of the hackle.

My preferred rods for skater fishing range from 8 to 10½ feet long. If I hit the stream specifically for skaters, I force myself to take a longer rod than I normally prefer. Line weights can range from 4 through 9, with 6- and 7-weight outfits doing the best job. Skaters are very wind-resistant and create havoc with a too-light line and leader. They can be cast with short rods but this is a decided handicap.

I rarely use a leader that is tapered lighter than 2X (except in one instance I will mention later). With the largest spiders even 0X and 1X can be used. The last time I asked Bebe about catching big fish on the spiders, he admitted to catching fish weighing up to 16 pounds; he may have passed that by now. You may have to experiment to see which leader lengths and tapers work best for you. I dress the entire leader with a paste-type floatant such as Miricilin. I prefer this to the stickier pure-silicone dressings. The intent is to keep the entire leader on the surface so the fly is not pulled under on the retrieve. If the skater becomes submerged the hackles start to lie back along the shank and the fly will not skim correctly.

One of the best ways to fish a skater is to drift it over a feeding trout just like any other dry fly. This will take trout, but giving the fly a tip-toe skating action will result in even more fish. To quote the late John Atherton, an artist and devoted fly fisherman, "A spider fished like any other dry fly will take trout, but a spider skated across a pool is deadly."

Hooking a fish on the original #16 skater requires special attention. After many, many misses on fish that actually inhaled the fly (rather than merely splashed at it), I found that a slight delay in setting the hook works better. However, my percentage of hooked fish is always better on spiders tied to larger hooks. There are various retrieve techniques for spiders, so each angler should experiment with a number of these to find the ones that work best for him or her. Norm, Tommy, and Joe preferred to cast across and slightly upstream and start the retrieve as soon as the fly hit the water. They retrieved by stripping the line a foot or so at a time in a very quick cadence. Right-hand casters should hold the line between the thumb and forefinger of their rod hands and retrieve by pulling the line with their left hands. I have watched Norm demonstrate this technique many times;

he holds the rod low but always at an angle to the line so the rod does not point directly at the fly. This right angle allows the fish to mouth the fly, and the rod tip can be used as a spring. This will give a better hooking percentage than when it is pointed directly at the fly. Holding the rod low is an advantage in windy weather, but I prefer a high-rod retrieve with as much line off the water as possible because this adds inducement to keep the fly on tippy toes; the fly appears to skate, bounce, and dance in a lighter manner when the rod is held high.

Cast these spiders up and across, straight across, or slightly down and across. Casting directly upstream or downstream does not work well. I fish my spiders more slowly than do most of my angling friends but, while my tempo is slower, I give the fly an extra bounce or two with a slight twitch of the rod tip. Remember to keep the line at a right angle to the rod.

Skater spiders work well on fairly flat pools; the attractive skating wake of the fly is more apparent to the fish. Of course, the fly can be fished in good pocket water if you fish with a short line. When fishing this way, I look for the flash of an active fish and skim the fly over apparent holding spots – in front of and behind obstructions, near patches of foam, along undercut banks, or anywhere experience tells me a fish could be waiting.

The pools on western rivers are sometimes hundreds of yards long. Since I prefer the across and slightly upstream cast and retrieve, I usually ease into the water at the tail of the pool and slowly proceed upstream. I might cover cruising fish or just make blind casts, looking for the hot spots within the pool, such as log or rock obstructions, or any possible cover affording the fish some protection from predators. Usually, the first cast and retrieve is the most productive, so I seldom make more than one or two casts to the same spot.

Big skaters are also quite effective in ponds. If I see cruising fish, I try to intercept their paths with a skimming fly. This can be exciting, especially in a pond with large trout. If no fish are showing, I bracket my casts to cover the pond as I proceed along the bank. In ponds holding skittish fish, I feel that a slight breeze is a distinct advantage – more to conceal my human scent than to add action to the fly.

I worked on one last facet of skater fishing recently. I tied a half-dozen #16 spiders with a smaller hackle, the diameter of a quarter instead of the usual fifty-cent-piece diameter. Because there was less wind resistance, I could use 4X tippets. And since I was showing these fish something radically different, I took trout that were virtually untouchable with the standard flies and methods. It works! Try the miniskaters along with the big ones.

There are many days in a fly fisher's life and too few hours to spend fishing, so when I'm out on a hot, sunny day and the trout are not active – when even the terrestrials are nonproductive – I often put on a Skater Spider to pick up the action.

Addendum: Since I wrote this chapter, I have had the pleasure and thrill of meeting and fishing with Bebe Anchorena. We fished together on the famous *Chimehuin* and *Traful* of Patagonia, Argentina. In the fly-tying den of Bebe's summer home there is a mounted trout of gargantuan proportions. "How big, Bebe?" I asked. "Over sixteen pounds," was his reply. "What did you take him on?" As a smile crossed his sunburned face he replied, "One of your Skater Spiders." What more can I say?

Chapter 9

The Flies
TROUT LOVE TO CHEW

An oversized Letort brown trout with dime-size spots stalked my fly with the deliberation of a hungry cougar. "Better than two feet long," I told myself. The special streamer wiggled in an up-and-down motion as it inched its dark flat sculpin-shaped body closer and closer to where I knelt in the tall grass. I stopped my retrieve to give the burly fish time to catch up to the fly. The fly settled to the bottom in a sculpinlike manner, and the trout closed in. An almost imperceptible twitch of my rod tip moved the fly ever so slightly, triggering a rush from the big brown who engulfed the sculpin with a ferocity that caused me to overreact. As I struck, the fly flew out of the fish's mouth and back over my head. Immediately, the enraged brown charged in the direction of the disappearing fly. As a result of its ferocious rush the fish slid partway up on the sloping bank, leaving itself high and dry. It floundered there an instant, then reentered the water. As the trout started to swim away, I plopped the fly just ahead of him and damn if he didn't grab it. This time the hook sank into the bony jaw and I "had the tiger by the tail." After such a flurry of activity,

105

the actual playing and landing of the big fish was anticlimactic. I had "sculpinated" another trout.

Sculpinating is a term I've coined to describe the way I entice trout to strike my own imitation of the sculpin: Old Ugly, my affectionate name for the Shenk Sculpin. The term *sculpinating* describes a method of fishing that mesmerizes a trout, sometimes causing the fish to cast caution to the wind as it attempts to pursue and engulf the wiggling fly undulating by. Old Ugly and its relatives are described in this chapter chronologically, through the progress of their development.

Marabou streamers, especially the white ones, have been favorites of mine since junior high school. Over the seasons, I have probably caught more large trout on marabous than on all other streamers combined. Their effectiveness may be attributed to the fibers that are constantly in motion, even when the fly is dead-drifting. Therefore, the marabou feather became one material necessary for the chewy flies.

The Fledermaus Streamer, originated by the late Bill Schneider, a western angler, became another one of my favorites. I first used it as a night fly, with tremendous success, and later found it worked just as well in daytime fishing. I was impressed with the number of fish that would grab the fly and lie there chewing on it. The ordinary fly was inhaled and rejected very quickly, but the Fledermaus, with its thick, soft body of muskrat fur, was often chewed on for seconds before being spit out. Even during the brightest part of summer days it was possible to lure large trout from their shadowy hangouts with a jumbo-size Fledermaus. I'm sure they mistook it for a crayfish, and, as in eating a natural "crawdad," the trout would pounce on the fly, bite it as if to immobilize it, reject it, and return just as quickly to bite it again.

Although not all fish are hooked on a Fledelmaus for the same reason, the greater number of strikes usually assures me of as great or greater total catch than with conventional streamers. One day a number of years ago, I was fishing "Paradise" on Spring Creek in central Pennsylvania. These catch-and-release fish can be most exasperating at times, but when a fly is hot with them, it's really hot. For the first two hours of the morning I moved a trout on every cast with a large Fledermaus; some fish were not much larger than the fly, and others were quite respectable. Even though the marabous and Fledermauses are first-rate flies on their own, it seemed inevitable that a thick, juicy-bodied fly would eventually be combined with the constantly moving marabou to create a series of new and quite effective patterns. The initial pattern was simple; a white marabou tail for action, and a juicy cream-colored fur body for a general minnowlike appearance. The fur chenille, or fur-loop, method of tying was used to create the thick body, which was then trimmed to give the fly the general shape of a minnow. This method of tying a fur body is unique, because the body can be trimmed to the desired shape without destroying the soft fleshlike feel. As far as I know, I was the first to use this trimming method, and described it several years later in *Garcia Fishing Annual 1975*.

My first use of this new pattern resulted in fooling two trout, both more than 18 inches long. Both came from undercut banks at my feet, and both inhaled the fly as they would a natural minnow. Since it was mid-August, and due to my love of dry-fly fishing, the new pattern was used only on occasion to fish spots where the terrestrial dries wouldn't entice a fish to the surface. One of my favorite methods was to ease the fly into the water downstream and swim it tail-first to a likely looking spot. Occasionally it only required four or five raisings and lowerings of the rod tip before a trout darted out and nailed the fly. When you fish the same streams over and over, as I do, you get to know the location of many individual trout. If I fished a spot I knew was a trout hideout and the usual method wouldn't work, I sometimes lowered the fly to the bottom, moving it at odd intervals. "Just like a nearly dead minnow," I would tell myself. It would take willpower on the part of the trout to refuse the fly.

The first modification of the soft-bodied fly came the following winter. I decided to add a marabou wing to it; to some I added white, to others brown. They were then put away until the spring trout season was well under way. The occasion first arose to try the new fly while I was poking along the Yellow Breeches, picking up an occasional trout on nymphs. As I paused to rest my weary bones, I noticed a commotion not too far from shore. There, a handsome hook-jawed brown slowly cruised, looking for trouble. I eased into casting position and flipped the nymph upstream from the trout. I tensed as the fly drifted past, but the burly trout ignored it, as he did a succession of accurate casts. "Maybe he wants a mouthful," I mused. My gaze rested on the new fly – the one with the brown wing – so, with a "nothing ventured, nothing gained" attitude, I quickly tied it to the

4X tippet. The fly was lowered into the water and squeezed like a sponge to free the trapped air and moisten down the body and the marabou. The first cast was way behind the fish, but he must have sensed it because he turned and swiftly charged the sinking fly. I gave the fly one feeble twitch and the big fish engulfed the artificial and attempted to swallow it. The ensuing battle was almost a letdown, as is often the case, and soon I was admiring a handsome male brown just over 20 inches long. I kept him out of water just long enough to photograph him, then put him back where he belonged.

A few weeks later, after many successes and a few failures, I demonstrated the fly for Dr. Howard "Howdy" Hoffman of Chambersburg, Pennsylvania. Howdy tied a couple of the brown marabous that evening, and tried them the following day. His first fish, a 21½-inch Falling Spring brown was handsome enough to be kept for mounting. Later in the day he went to the Conococheague Creek and landed another male, also 21½ inches long.

Probably the most effective imitation of the entire series is the Old Ugly. Although the wingless white streamer and the marabou wing are suggestive of the more common minnows, such as the dace and the shiner, Old Ugly was designed and shaped to suggest a sculpin, that broad-headed minnow commonly referred to as a "muddler," "miller's thumb," or "bullhead." The Muddler Minnow streamer is probably the most effective sculpin pattern ever devised, along with the newer Spuddler and the Whitlock Sculpin. The Shenk Sculpin series is not designed to replace any of these, but rather to supplement them. The fly is tied with a marabou tail, with a soft, fur body tied Fledermaus-style and trimmed in a broad tapering shape common to the sculpin, and finished with a broad, flat, deer-hair head.

My first experiences with the Shenk Sculpin were both pleasant and surprising, not only from a standpoint of numbers but also from the size of the fish. Of course, it is difficult to keep a good thing secret, so after a few teasing sessions with a couple of my good fishing buddies, I showed them the patterns and the tying procedure. Once again, as so often happens, the pupils outdid the teacher. In one episode Terry Ward, of Chambersburg, Pennsylvania, had forsaken his local Falling Spring for a morning's fishing on the Letort. Both, as you know, are famous limestoners, but the Letort

has the reputation for giving up an occasional giant brown. I had described to Terry my success in the Quarry Meadow the week before, where I fished downstream to the railroad bridge with the new sculpin, then, after a lengthy pause, fished back up toward the quarry with a Letort Cricket. Terry said he planned the very same procedure. The idea was a sound one, but fate has a way of playing tricks; this time fate was more than generous.

Terry methodically probed one pocket, then another, with the black sculpin, catching and releasing an occasional trout. Presently, he was confronted by a large willow tree under which the water flowed swiftly, dark and inviting. The fly entered the water with a tiny plop and, as it sank, drifted out of sight into the unknown. "Snagged," Terry grumbled as he felt heavy resistance on the line. But the snag came to life, and with a heart-thumping surge an enormous trout hog-wallowed the surface. Terry didn't know it then, but every trout fisherman's dream was about to come true for him. For ten minutes the trout bore upstream, diving into one weed bed after another. It was not the spectacular reel-screeching run of a fear-crazed salmon, but the slow, powerful surging of a well-fed brown trout. The fish tired little by little, then, in a last-ditch effort, turned and plowed downstream through a logjam. Terry followed, and with a little manipulation, laced the line through the jam. There was no beaching this monster, so Terry made a quick decision. He entered the frigid water and wrestled the fish into the grass. Shivering from cold water and excitement, a wet Terry Ward admired a brown trout 29½ inches long, weighing 10½ pounds! This was the trophy of a lifetime.

I have had numerous opportunities to fish these sculpins in western rivers such as the Firehole, Yellowstone, Madison, and Big Hole; they were effective in each. A stormy, overcast day on the upper Yellowstone River comes to mind. It was early September, more windy than usual, and the cutthroats were not moving. We did catch a few baby fish, but could not interest any of the larger fish we could see in the clear water. I went through a series of unsuccessful flies before tying on a black Shenk Sculpin. That didn't interest the one large cutt I was playing with, so I finally used a sneaky trick I had occasionally been successful with in the past. I let the fly drift into a patch of moss about two feet from the trout's head, where it promptly hung up. I twitched it ever so slightly, moving fly and moss at the same time. The trout was on it in a millisecond, and I reacted so hard the fly was jerked from the fish's mouth. Immediately I cast again, used the same maneuver, and latched on to a powerhouse of a cutthroat. Minutes later, a 20-inch male fish was reposing on the gravel. The wind then picked up again and the fishing came to another standstill; my 3½-pound fish was the only good one for the day.

Lest you think all my forays end in success, let me mention a few "unsuccessful" successes, the kind where I'm fortunate enough to move and hook a large fish, but for one reason or another do not land it.

I can still see the yard-long rainbow rising up from the depths of a deep hole on the Madison to clamp down on my largest Old Ugly, a 5-inch-long fly tied to a 1/0 hook. A reel-screeching run terminating in a tremendous leap is my only memory of this wonderful fish, because seconds later we parted company when he dove into a tangle of underwater roots and broke the 1X leader.

Nor will I forget the gigantic brown from a nameless lake farther north in Montana. I cast the sculpin out as far as I could, hoping it would settle in about twenty-five feet of water. It settled perhaps five feet when my line started to peel off at a steady rate. I set the hook firmly and then held on for fifteen minutes. This fish was big and I knew it. I sweated blood and my wrist ached, but gradually the pressure of the little rod took its toll. The fish was wallowing now, and steadily I worked him closer to a spot where he could be wrestled onto the bank. Slowly, the biggest hook-jawed brown I'd ever seen cruised past me. Constant pressure from the side turned the fish in decreasing circles. I felt the tiny bump as my line-leader connection passed into my rod guides. "Just a little more," I muttered, as I eased my hand into the water, "just a little more." I really didn't know what I was going to do, or how I was going to do it. I just knew this fish was too big for the dinky net I normally used for fish up to 2 feet in length. The great brown opened his mouth one last time and the fly came free. Pausing momentarily, he slowly disappeared into the depths. My breath was released with an audible *whooosh*, and I stood shaking. I might have cried a little, but I'll never tell. That giant old brown has died of old age by now. I never saw him again.

To some of my friends I'm a short-rod nut, and I readily admit a decided preference for little rods. Lately, most of my serious sculpin fishing is done with a wispy 6½-foot graphite rod, but I have used the shorter fiberglass rods, and occasionally one of my pet bamboo rods. I prefer graphite for sculpin fishing, though; my most frequently used rods handle both 3-weight and 4-weight lines. The light, delicate rods call for hooks that are as sharp as possible for better penetration.

Many times during a fishing day I'll shift from nymph to dry fly to sculpin, and back again. I generally use a 4X tippet for the sculpin and a 5X for the others. If I cut back to a 3X or a 2X for sculpinating a particularly large fish, I tie my way back up to the 5X for my smaller flies. Naturally, the 6Xs and even the 7Xs have to be used when fishing the tiny midges. Long tippets are needed in the 24- to 30-inch class; when it gets shorter than 24 inches I replace it. A longer tippet has more stretch, which cushions the strike better than a short tippet can.

Any attempt to cast a well-weighted sculpin with the same casting cadence you'd use on a regular dry or wet fly will cause trouble. The secret of casting these rascals is to make a softer cast, allowing the fly to straighten the line and leader before coming forward with a somewhat slow sweep of the rod. Hours of tossing line for smallmouth bass weighted with soft crayfish and other delicate goodies in my younger years gave me the needed timing for tossing the sculpin around. It is difficult to describe but easy to demonstrate. Unless I'm really reaching for a fish, I prefer to stop the rod tip fairly high as the fly hits the water.

Techniques for fishing the sculpin are varied, even from cast to cast. One of my favorite methods, and probably the most deadly, is to cast the Shenk Sculpin upstream, allow it to sink to the bottom, then bounce it downstream in short and long hops, always keeping the fly fairly close to the bottom. The fly darts up from the bottom and then descends again. When I slack off the line to allow the descent, I try to maintain contact with the fly so that any "take" will be transmitted up the line. This is such an unusual presentation that the large trout really fall for it. I have had the trout actually swallow the sculpin on more than one occasion. Recently, at one of the Allenberry Fishing School at which Joe Humphreys and I teach, this method accounted for a big brown, nearly 23 inches long, from a pocket of water that had been fished constantly all morning.

A variation of this retrieve is preferably done in an area with a silt or marl bottom. In this presentation, the off-the-bottom twitch is very slight, so the fly makes only a feeble move but shoots up a small, visible puff of mud. This can fool even the most cautious trout. One day when I was fishing a tiny meadow stream under a bright midday sun, I cast, searching out all suspected hiding spots. Needless to say, this short-range fishing calls for a quiet soft-treading approach, and be careful that no shadows cross the trout's location. I worked every spot that looked even halfway fishy. On one very short cast, I dropped the fly at the mouth of an underwater muskrat hole. I pumped the rod tip ever so gently. The fly inched off the bottom in a tiny puff of silt, and before it had a chance to completely settle I was hanging on to nearly four pounds of infuriated brown trout. The fly was nearly out of sight in the maw of this big fish; luckily, the barbless hook was removed without drawing blood. Weeks later I caught the same fish again, using a Letort Cricket.

I occasionally use a cross-stream cast when attempting to place the fly slightly upstream from my quarry. As the fly hits the water I tense for a quick strike. If there is no fast hit, I swim the fly back to me with the marabou tail doing its darndest to wiggle up a strike. I like to drop the fly right next to the bank, against a log, or roots, or up under the brush. Accuracy is extremely important; dropping the fly exactly where it should be placed is one of the secrets of fly-fishing success. This is edge-fishing at its finest, whether the edge is as just described or where two currents merge.

Knowing where to cast the fly is an art. I try to drop the fly close to areas where a trout is hiding, resting, or feeding. I realize that this encompasses many possibilities, but it is this variety that provides intrigue. Understandably, I sometimes do better on home streams where daily fishing has revealed some of these hiding spots to me. Trout are creatures of habit and, if left undisturbed in their daily routines, will feed at the same locations every day. They will also retreat to the same hiding spots unless disturbed by a larger fish, a predator, or some other nuisance. I sometimes spook fish that are holding in a particular spot. With a memory as poor as mine, I might repeat the same mistake on a second visit, but seldom do I make the same mistake the third time. By then, I'm usually ready to get a fly to the trout if he is in an accessible position.

Whenever possible I work in closely, and fish with a very short line. It is more enjoyable when I can watch the fly and observe the trout as it takes. Close-in fishing, no matter which fly you are using, calls for stealth: no heavy tromping or careless wading. I try to approach the trout with the sun at my back as long as I'm not putting my shadow where it can be seen by the trout.

There is another technique called the "crayfish twitch," in which I attempt to simulate the action of a fleeing crayfish. This is quite a retrieve, jerking the rod tip while trying to keep the fly in a confined area. It resembles moving like crazy without getting anywhere. The best way to learn this retrieve is to watch a live crayfish in its jerky flight to safety. In streams with many crayfish this is an extremely successful method. What do we care if the sculpin is taken for a minnow or a crawdad, as long as it is taken? I have had trout follow the fly in a "ho-hum" manner until the fly started to dance like a scared crayfish. Then the "ho-hum" attitude quickly changed and I would tense for a very fast strike.

Still another tactic I use calls for very steady nerves. Trout, particularly large ones, are intrigued by following the fly at a safe distance, but they pace themselves so they never quite close the gap. I stop my retrieve in these cases, and permit the fly to descend in a natural manner. Curiosity will usually cause the fish to nose the fly, but just before the trout touches it I pull it out of his reach. This procedure must usually be repeated two or three times before the fish gets agitated enough to rush the fly. If the fish does not turn away on the first pull, a strike is usually guaranteed, and it will probably be a savage one. I generally overreact at this point, but that's one of the things that makes fly fishing so much fun. It is easy to strike too hard, and with a very short line something will surely give: sometimes it is a broken leader, sometimes a smashed rod.

Tactics and techniques can vary from pool to pool and from cast to cast. There are some locations where, because of overhead cover, the best way for the fly to be seen is for you to swim the fly downstream, tail first. Maintain a tight line and ease the sculpin under any obstructions; if there is no strike on the drift back, allow the fly to hang in the current momentarily before it is twitched back upstream. Bring it upstream a foot or so, drop it back again, then repeat this a few times. Don't waste too much time in one spot.

Another tidbit well worth mentioning is the approach and retreat. It is only common sense to be as quiet as possible when approaching a trout's lair, but what happens when a promising lie fails to produce a fish? I ease away as quietly as I approached. I don't want a good fish to see my fly and then associate it with the vibration of footsteps as I move on. Think about it.

Chapter 10

Jewel Of
THE HEADWATERS

The fly line zipped behind me once, lengthening my cast, and then shot forward. The tiny barbless Letort Cricket dropped to the water's surface, floated a few inches, and disappeared in a splashy rise. I set the hook and was rewarded with the tug of a surprised trout. A moment later, I gently released the fish.

A common occurrence on a typical trout stream? Wrong! The stream I was fishing was the mountainous headwaters of a well-known Pennsylvania trout stream. I was in a tunnel of rhododendron and mountain laurel, rather than in the open for pleasurable casting. My backcast had to be so accurate that it propelled the fly into a tiny opening in the brush. The forward cast had to deliver the fly over a log, under an overhanging limb, and still hit the water within inches of my target.

Seeking natives in the headwaters is a rewarding facet of fly fishing if trout size is not important, but from a casting standpoint it can be so frustrating that only a handful of anglers ever consider it. But if you don't explore mountain brooklets you may never see a true native brookie with

117

its red- or orange-laced fins, tiny red spots with halos of blue, or tiny blue spots with halos of cream or yellow. This, coupled with the wormlike vermiculations across the back, gives you the most beautiful fish in existence. The quest for the disappearing native is also unusual because you seldom see another angler. As a matter of fact, when you do see a parked vehicle by the stream you travel on to get away from the crowded conditions. Forget this type of fishing if you crave the companionship of kindred souls, and travel to a popular stream like the Letort or Yellow Breeches. If your only desire is to make graceful casts with a long fly rod and tie into a heavy trout measured in pounds rather than inches, then pass by the little mountain streams. If not, read on.

Years ago, when fishermen used long rods for all their fly fishing, 9-footers were touted for mountain fishing. The idea was to extend the rod through the bushes and drop the fly on the water without spooking the fish. It worked fine in theory, but trying to push or drag the rod through the brush was a headache. As an answer, I gradually decreased the length of my mountain rods and now carry a flexible one-piece fiberglass rod between 5 and 5½ feet long. I have a number in this category because I finish almost all my rods from blanks, and reduce the hardware and rod-grip size in proportion.

Flexibility is necessary to load the rod on even a very short cast. (Sometimes only the leader is extended beyond the rod tip.) My mountain rods are designed to cast a 4-weight line, either double-tapered or weight-forward. The weight-forward capabilities are seldom realized in small-stream fishing because most casts range from seven to twenty feet or so. To balance these diminutive rods, my preferred reels are the tiny Hardy Flyweight and the Orvis CFO II.

I usually fish with 10- to 12-foot leaders on more open water, such as the Letort or Falling Spring. My mountain leaders are scaled-down versions designed to turn over properly at close range. These are seldom longer than 9 feet. I have no set formula for short leaders, except to tie and retie until they turn over the way I want them to. Butt sections are seldom more than .017 inches, and I tip out at 4X or 5X, usually the latter. These shorter leaders seem to turn over better if the tippet is no longer than 20 inches, even though tippets of 24 inches are used more often. I dislike a line-to-leader connection that hangs up in the rod guides when I'm taking line in or out, so I use the epoxy splice exclusively in this fishing. If you haven't tried this connection, you should, not only for mountain brook fishing but for all your trout fishing. I have never had one fail.

Mountain trout are hungry trout, so any pattern works well as long as it isn't too large. My favorite dries are primarily terrestrial patterns: the Letort Cricket, Letort Hopper, and the floating ants. The advantage of the hopper and cricket patterns, with their deer-hair heads, is their floatability. Nothing is as disappointing to me as a fly that requires constant drying and redressing in order for it to continue floating. I prefer the flies in #26 for these patterns because most trout taken will be small, seldom exceeding 9 inches in length. I dislike the very small flies because a fooled headwater fish is a voracious feeder and will inhale the tiny fly way too deep. On occasion, I fish small streamers, preferably marabous, in pools where I feel there may be a good fish skulking beneath a jumble of roots, an undercut bank, or a logjam.

During the summer I have waded wet in sneakers and an old pair of jeans. This is refreshing perhaps, but potentially dangerous too. Because of the possibility of encountering a poisonous snake, wearing hip boots is a prudent choice, although in all the years I have fished mountain waters, I have encountered only five poisonous snakes, and only once did I have a close call.

I was fishing the headwaters of a mountain stream an hour's drive from my Carlisle, Pennsylvania, home one mid-July day when the snake encounter occurred. For two weeks the weather had been hot and dry, a condition that lures snakes to the cooler surroundings along the water. The section I was fishing was densely overgrown, so I climbed out of the water often to move from pool to pool. I was tired, so I let down my guard, forgetting about reptiles. Through the tangled mess ahead I could see an inviting pool with a rising trout, so I grabbed a limb with my right hand to climb the bank. An odd feeling made me glance up directly into the beady eyes of a rattler coiled about two feet from my forearm. The snake was not large, but at that point it looked like a python. With as little motion as possible I eased my arm back and retreated homeward, forgetting the pool and its rising trout. I have not forgotten the lesson: Look before you step or reach. If you dislike snakes, forget headwater-fishing in states where rattlers and copperheads are found.

During the summer, I prefer early-morning fishing because I can usually be sure that another fisherman has not preceded me. Headwaters trout are forever hungry, but they are spooky; only the first fisherman of the day finds undisturbed fish. The trout are seldom selective, and a careful approach and cast will generally result in a rise, assuming, of course, that the fish sees the fly. Approach is much more important than the type of fly being used, but the first presentation must be a good one, and accompanied by a drag-free float. Of course, I have many times crawled to a pool, negotiated the correct casting position, and hooked my fly on a twig or limb on the initial cast. In this case, I retrieve the fly and proceed to the next pool. I have also added knee pads to my mountain outfit to save a lot of wear and tear on my fragile hippers. I use the kind that concrete finishers recommend.

Early morning fishing has other bonuses, too. Unless it has been an exceptionally hot night, stinging- and biting-insect activity is diminished, although a good insect repellent should always be part of every fisherman's equipment; one of the "after-bite" solutions is a good item to have along for immediate relief from itching. Animal life is also more active in the early-morning hours. I may have the pleasure of seeing a deer or two, a wild turkey, grouse, fox, or raccoon. Muskrats are commonplace, and I have even seen a mink on occasion.

Although morning fishing is my favorite, I seldom pass up a chance to fish in the afternoon or evening, too. A few seasons ago I got the sudden urge for some headwater fishing. I had a spot on one stream in particular in mind. I quickly packed my outfit in the van, added a small cooler of soft drinks, some sharp cheese and pretzels, and was on my way. The city day was hot and uncomfortable, but as I cruised across the mountains there was a decided coolness to the air. How refreshing! I eased the van into a shady spot beside the tiny stream and slipped into my hip waders and a lightweight vest. I often wear a fly box on my chest, but not this time.

On my very first cast the little cricket imitation landed and disappeared in the spray of a trout's take. A 14-inch brown danced around the tiny pool. After a short battle, I admired the trout and released it. As I proceeded upstream, I landed and released five more browns and one rainbow, all between 12 and 14 inches long. These fish had undoubtedly moved into the headwaters from hatchery stocking far downstream be-

cause no stocking is done in these fragile headwaters. Trout fishing is all relative; in these tiny waters the fish were comparable to 18- and 20-inch fish taken in the bigger streams near home. I don't feel that catching a 6- to 12-inch fish from confined waters is any less enjoyable than taking an 18-incher on bigger waters. As a matter of fact, in some of these mountain streams the natives seldom reach the minimum legal size except during the fall, when larger fish move into the brooklets to spawn; a number of these streams will produce fish from 7 to 9 inches long. A 10-inch native here would be a real trophy to be admired, photographed, released, and then bragged about. As I have mentioned, even though these headwater fish are perpetually hungry, they are also easily spooked. A careful approach is in order, so I wear dull nonreflective clothing, preferably brown or green, and make sure nothing shines to flash a telltale signal to the trout. Unless it's an extremely overcast day, I also remove my wristwatch.

Experience dictates that I concentrate on the tail of the pool first. In the past, when I ignored the shallow tail of the pool, I invariably spooked fish while trying to position myself for a good shot at the head. When an alarmed fish charges through the pool, there is nothing to do but move on. If my initial casts in the tail do not produce a rise, I'll generally give the midpool area a shot, then concentrate on the head, where the water drops in from upstream. Aside from food, the fish's main concern is safety. If the boss of the pool is lying in the tailwater and something threatens or alarms him, he only has to shoot upstream to his protective cover – an undercut bank or overhanging rock. The same fish at the upper end of the pool has to turn downstream for its protective cover. "Then why are the fish not always at the lower end of the pool?" you ask. As summer progresses, the water warms, depleting its oxygen content; but the aerated water tumbling in from upstream adds needed oxygen, hence the position change. At other times, the "big boy" may have moved up to gulp additional insects during a particularly intense hatch. In this case, the fish is sacrificing safety. Therefore, hit the bottom of the pool first; if there are no takers, go to the middle. If there are still no takers, cast to the extreme head of the pool.

In the past few years I have hunted deer extensively in Virginia and Pennsylvania. Virginia headwater brookie streams are much more open than are the rhododendron-canopied ones I fish near home. A longer rod can be used without the continual annoyance of a rod tip caught in the brush. The longer 7-, 7½-, and 8-foot rods may be fished successfully in these streams.

Although most of my headwater experience is in Pennsylvania, enjoyable headwaters-fishing exists in almost every state trout inhabit. The tiny brooks of New England harbor many natives. Many of the brown trout and rainbow trout waters of the Midwest have native brookies to the bitter end. I have had enjoyable brookie fishing in the West, mainly Wyoming and Montana waters; and the true native of the West can be found in the High Plains brooklets. These cutthroats are bright, colorful fish and can be every bit as exasperating as any other native if approached incorrectly.

Catching a big trout does not always define an enjoyable fishing trip. Some of my most pleasant memories are of infrequent little encounters with headwater trout in early autumn. The leaves are changing colors, the sky is a deep blue, and the afternoons are pleasantly mild. The brookies are in their spawning colors and even more splendid than normal. This is a great time to be afield, and is even more rewarding when you catch and admire one of the jewels of the headwaters.

Chapter 11

TERRESTRIALS

Terrestrial fishing and terrestrial patterns go back almost to the genesis of fly fishing, but it wasn't until the late 1940s that "terrestrial" became a household word. Joe Brooks called the development of terrestrials "a revolution in fly fishing." His first article about terrestrial fishing featured the Charlie Fox-Vince Marinaro fishing team, and introduced the Jassid pattern to the general fly-fishing public. Published in the late 1950s, the article introduced an entirely new concept for many fishermen from coast to coast. Dry-fly fishing had previously emphasized matching mayfly hatches and other aquatic insects, but long before Brooks's article on the Jassid appeared in print, some of us in the Carlisle, Pennsylvania, area had already been fishing terrestrial patterns and using special techniques, primarily on the Letort. As a matter of fact, the first fly I ever tied, in around 1940, was a Hard-bodied Black Ant.

Charlie Fox coined the term "terrestrial" to encompass the numerous land-based insects that reach the water more by accident than by design; these include ants, crickets, beetles, grasshoppers, leafhoppers (Jassids), and inchworms. Of lesser importance, but also valuable to the fly fisher, are bees, houseflies, caterpillar moths, and locusts.

Since the 1940s there has been a definite evolution in terrestrial tackle brought on by the newer rod materials such as fiberglass, graphite, and boron. I use graphite rods that throw 3- and 4-weight lines for most of my terrestrial trouting. Graphite rods have the wonderful ability to perform well with more than one line weight. I have fished with a double-taper 3-weight line instead of the 4-weight on many calm days. The 3-weight's more delicate presentation often makes the difference between a successful day and one that is just so-so. If I had to choose one rod (heaven forbid) for this fishing, I'd take a 6½-foot graphite rod with a 3- or-4-weight line. There are many good rod brands on the market but my 6½-footers are the Orvis Flea and the Gary Loomis, in both the regular graphite and IM6.

By far, the majority of terrestrial fishermen prefer single-action reels as opposed to the heavier automatics or multipliers. In the past few years there has been a marked increase in the number of single-action reels on the market manufactured by companies in England, Japan, and Argentina, as well as the United States. For my tiniest, lightest rods I lean toward little reels under three inches in diameter and weighing less than three ounces. Slightly longer and heavier rods balance better with larger, heavier reels.

Another consideration when choosing a reel is how much backing is needed for strong-winded fish. If you fish areas where trout might run into the backing, by all means go to a slightly larger-diameter reel that will hold the line plus the needed backing. Although backing is seldom needed, it is nice to have. My western reels are equipped with adequate backing because the trout in the large western streams can have a great deal of stamina. Be sure also to have a smooth backing-to-line connection so it won't hang in the guides on the way in or out. I use a nail knot coated with Pliobond for a smooth connection.

I use a floating line and switch between double-tapered and weight-forward tapered lines. The rule of thumb is, if you are making casts over forty feet long, go with the weight-forward taper; if most of your casting will be in the twenty- to thirty-foot range, a double-tapered line works well and you can reverse it whenever one end shows excessive wear, so you actually get two lines for the price of one.

A variety of tapered leaders are available. The George Harvey formulas, popularized by both George and his friend Joe Humphreys, are excellent—I use them often in various lengths. I never go heavier than .017 inches for my leader butts. I attach the hard nylon butt to the tip of my line with an epoxy splice. Then, using a variety of leader types, including a Harvey formula, and sometimes a medium-stiff knotless tapered leader, I find the .016 diameter section near the butt-end of the knotless tapered leader, slip it off, and attach it to the permanent .017 section. At the tip end, I cut it at the .007 diameter point and tie my favorite 4X (.007) tippet material to this. If I go to 5X (.006), I usually cut the 4X back slightly to get better leader turnover. The tippet section is usually 24 to 30 inches long. When the tippet gets to be shorter than 20 inches, I cut it off and replace it with a longer one.

Don't be afraid to experiment a little on leader types and materials. Part of the fun in this game is doing some thinking for yourself. Except when using the tiniest ants and beetles, I seldom go finer than 5X. Over the past few seasons I have successfully used 4X tippets when fishing the crickets, hoppers, and ants. On days when the trout are finicky, I go back to the longer 5X tippets and things usually pick up again.

My top terrestrial pattern choice, for a number of reasons, is a Letort Cricket. First, it's easy to tie, and it's a good floater, which enables me to catch numerous fish without changing flies. The cricket catches trout everywhere; I have used it in the East, South, and West, and others say it has been successful for them in Europe, the British Isles, India, Africa, and New Zealand. A number of years ago Lefty Kreh told me he had a ball on the Traun, where the grayling went crazy over it. It has become a universal pattern.

Grasshoppers are a must in any terrestrial fisherman's fly box. I lean toward the flat-winged Shenk Hopper, which I also call the Letort Hopper. Coincidentally, Ernie Schweibert contrived a terrific hopper pattern also called the Letort Hopper. Ernie's pattern started with a yellow-nylon-yarn body, matched but divided mottled turkey-quill wings (like the Joe's Hopper), and a clipped deer-hair head with tips extending to the rear. My pattern started with a pale yellow dubbed spun-fur body, and a mottled turkey wing with the feather folded, tied flat, and trimmed in a broad "V." The head is naturally tan deer hair, tied and clipped the same way as in

Ernie's pattern. So, while I was tying and fishing my Shenk Hopper on the upper Letort and showing it to very few other fishermen, Ernie made a few visits to Charlie Fox's meadow and showed the Schweibert Hopper to Ross Trimmer and Charlie. They promptly named his hopper the Letort Hopper. Everything in these patterns was a series of coincidences, and neither of us knew that our similar patterns had identical names. So I've added *Shenk* to my version of the Letort Hopper because I wouldn't want to be accused of pirating Ernie's fly. The Letort Cricket, which came about after the Letort Hopper and other hoppers began to be refused regularly, is my creation.

There are now scads of hopper patterns on the market, most of them very good. Pick one or two patterns—you don't need them all—in #14 and #16 hooks. I even prefer the smaller sizes in Wyoming and Montana, but it helps to have several big flies tucked away, just in case.

If I tied a pattern for every ant variety, I could start my own ant colony.

Basically, most ant fishing can be done with a few hook sizes, in black and cinnamon. The Fur Ant, consisting of two bulges of fur dubbing with a dry-fly hackle between them (at the waist), is a very easy pattern to tie, and a good floater, too. My second choice is a deer-hair ant first shown to me by Chauncy Lively in the early 1960s, but the drawback to this ant is its fragility. Even when coated with thinned goop, it becomes scraggly after being chewed by one or two fish. I consider the #16 black ant the work-horse, and the #18 cinnamon the best size. I carry the black ants in large and small sizes, a few #10s and some #20 to #28s. I carry cinnamons ranging in size from #18 to #28.

I also use two versions of deer-hair beetles. I use a black or brown beetle made of deer hair clipped to shape for the larger "June Bug ties." The Crowe Beetle, devised years ago by John Crowe, of Johnstown, Pennsylvania, has hollow deer hair tied in with the tips extending back past the bend of the hook. This extended hair is then pulled forward and tied off just behind the hook eye. The tips are clipped in a short "brush" to suggest a beetle's head. Like Chauncy's deer-hair ant, this tie is fragile and can be strengthened by saturating it with vinyl cement or thinned goop. A good brand of goop now on the market is Flexament.

The true Letort Beetle is another pattern in common use. This is a silhouette tie with a wing consisting of two cock ring-necked pheasant head or neck feathers cemented one on top of the other and trimmed in an oval shape. The feathers are then tied flat on top of the hook. The body of this pattern is a palmered hackle, trimmed top and bottom like its predecessor, Vince Marinaro's Jassid. I once landed two 20-inch Letort browns on #28 beetles during the course of one summer while I was doing research on the practicality of various patterns tied on the diminutive hooks.

Jassids are the famous little imitations of the leafhopper. They come in a variety of colors and abound on the stream edges during the hottest months. The flat wing of this pattern is tied with a jungle-cock eye feather or nail. Two other terrestrial patterns you might only use three or four times in your life are the seventeen year locust and the orange-and-black gypsy moth worm. During peak infestations the trout sometimes refuse these flies. Could you eat hot dogs three times a day for weeks on end?

Approaching a rising fish or its lair is extremely important. No matter how well you cast, a noisy approach alerts the fish to your presence before it even sees your imitation, eliminating your chance of catching it. Approaching fish from downstream is usually the best way to move. If you are wading, move slowly so you don't push waves ahead of you. Trout are nervous critters, and any quick movement, flash, or shadow can create the illusion of a predator moving in, so try to minimize unnatural movements. The underwater sound of rocks crunching as you wade also alerts fish. An unsuspecting fish is much easier to fool than an alerted one, so walk softly to minimize vibrations. I have taken many fish from just a few feet away by using the quiet, soft approach.

Shadows, silhouettes, and reflections are all danger signals for the fish and the fisherman. Approaching the stream with your body silhouetted against the sky will usually mean defeat even if you're the greatest caster in the world. If you must be silhouetted, crouch low and keep far enough behind the trout so he does not detect your presence. If possible, try to blend into the background by positioning a bush, tree, or other obstruction behind you to shield your outline from the fish.

I have noticed that certain sections of my favorite streams are most productive when fished at a particular time of day. The reflection of the sun seems to influence fishing. And reflection from a shiny piece of equipment or a rod with a shiny shaft can scuttle a quiet approach. My strategy is to hit streams during the daylight periods when the reflections won't precede me. On an overcast day I sometimes head for a favorite meadow at a time when I would not normally fish that piece of water. For instance, one favorite meadow of mine usually fishes best in the morning until about ten o'clock. From ten until three the sun throws reflections ahead of me, so I avoid the meadow during those hours unless the day is cloudy or rainy.

If a fish's vision is limited by the bank in one eye and the sun in the other, my chances of raising that fish are slim. My strategy is to cast to the small shady places and tiny spots where trout lie in shadow. If the opposite bank is shaded, it is usually more productive, though it may be more difficult to cast to. If you proceed upstream on or along the left bank and cast to the right bank, you'll find the casting easier.

Occasionally, because of brushy banks or other obstructions, you must fish from the right bank. Drift-casts, right-hand reverse-curve casts, or back-hand casts often work well in these situations. I often cast ahead on the bank, with just the leader or a portion of it on the water. If the sun is projecting your shadow too far ahead (as in early morning or late afternoon), fish another section of the stream. It is sometimes best to fish before the sun hits the water or after it has left. To sum up the approaches: minimize silhouettes, shadows, and reflections, and don't stomp.

Fishing the rise is exactly that – casting directly to rising fish. In most instances, these fish are taking a bite of food drifting past their feeding positions. They can be fooled on ant, Jassid, hopper, or cricket patterns. Usually, I cast with whatever pattern I happen to have on hand at the time. If it fails and the trout continue to feed, I check the water closely to see which insect they may have singled out. Ants may be swarming, or beetles are being blown into the water; whatever, I attempt to match the natural food. Only when the fish are very finicky is there a problem; some of these incessant feeders in catch-and-release waters are maddening. Just bear in mind that the rising trout are showing you where they are feeding and what food they prefer. The rest is up to you.

My favorite presentation, which often works on feeding fish, especially when they are moving to larger beetles, ants, crickets, or hoppers, is to cast the fly so it plops almost on the fish – seven or eight inches out from, and slightly behind, its eye. I try to obtain a reflexive response from the trout with this presentation because I have found through many years of experience that a fly delivered this way often causes the fish to turn and grab it without thinking. This is a conditioned reflex, much like raising your arm in defense when someone pushes a fist at you. I have demonstrated this to many people over the years, and it has now become one of the standard methods of fly fishing. Because larger terrestrials hit the water with a splash, you should overpower the cast to make the fly splat. The splat-cast works for feeding fish as well as for those that are hidden and waiting for food.

Fishing the water is the opposite of fishing the rise. It requires casting skill and fair eyesight, for you must be able to recognize hiding spots and feeding and resting spots to make your casts count. In meadow fishing I look for undercut banks, and if tall grass hangs out over the water the conditions are even better. I look for overhanging bushes, the forward edges of obstructions where food collects, and patches of foam that collect food and provide a protective curtain over the fish. A cricket or hopper dropped into the edge of this foam and jiggled slightly like a struggling insect can bring nerve-shattering strikes from good fish. Fish the edges — those places where there are current changes, lines between open water and slack currents, or spots where currents hit obstructions and glance off. You gain insight about edges only by years of experience gained on the stream by trying, doing, observing, and occasionally failing.

Bridges are also great places for terrestrials, and trout hide under them awaiting falling food.

One presentation I use is to cast over an obstruction to reach a particular spot. The obstruction may be a log, a patch of weeds, bankside grass, watercress, or a rock. I also cast over low footbridges if there is insufficient clearance under them. I stay back from the water's edge and cast out and over the grass or bank, watching my line for a telltale twitch indicating a rise, or listening for the strike. Then, I set the hook and reel myself toward the fish. If a hooked fish cannot be skated over the obstruction, I reel myself toward it and then release the fish. This tactic is not recommended in dangerously deep water or where the stream bottom is mucky, as in the Letort. As I proceed upstream, I look far enough ahead to pick out fishy-looking spots to cast to, and then decide just how to make my pitch. I may also spot a trout in a feeding position, ready-made for a "behind the eye" cast.

Regardless of the fly used, if you find a great trout actively feeding in an obviously hurried manner, get the fly to him as quickly as possible. Sometimes these feeding sprees are short and the fish will finish feeding before you get a match-the-hatch tied on. A large fish knows he is vulnerable in open water during daylight, so when he does feed, he shows himself only briefly.

A few years ago I was finishing a morning of terrestrial fishing on the Letort, when ahead of me the surface erupted with the swirl of a large trout feeding on minnows. Although I had on a midsize cricket, common sense dictated that I tie on a sculpin pattern. But experience told me to get on with it. Once, twice, I cast the cricket with negative results. The fish was still boiling the water. The third cast was beyond the trout and off to one side. Then I skimmed the fly like a streaking minnow, and immediately the big brown had it. After a spirited battle, the trout was ready for beaching. Just as I reached for it, he opened his mouth and disgorged an

8-inch brown; when I banked the fish, it disgorged yet another small trout. The big brown weighed over 6 pounds and was 26 inches long.

The patterns, tackle, and techniques that I have described certainly should enable you to get started as a successful terrestrial fisherman. Refinements in techniques and tackle will come to you as you gain experience in the wonderful world of trouting.

PART III

FLIES

Chapter 12

Fly PATTERNS

Certain tidbits of information regarding fly patterns were deliberately left out of the preceding chapters. The following consolidates these elements relating to materials, sizes, and pattern variations, and includes instructions on how to tie those that may differ somewhat.

Sulfurs

Sulfur is the common name for *Epeorus vitrea* and *Ephemerella dorothea*. According to Charlie Fox, at one time it was known as the Little Yellow Drake, and because of its sulfur color he began calling them Sulfurs. The name has stuck, though some still call it the Pale Evening Dun. However, the *pattern* known as the Pale Evening Dun was tied to imitate the *Ephemerella dorothea*, thus the name.

I wrote an article for *Fly Fisherman* magazine called "Sulfurs – Variations on a Theme," in which I described ten Sulfur dun and spinner imitations, all of which I have used successfully over the years to fool trout during the Sulfur hatch and spinner fall. The one predominant feature largely overlooked when tying Sulfurs is the orange color of the thorax; I think this feature is very important in the imitation. In tying each variation, I try to wrap the hackle so the underlying orange thorax is apparent. One of the patterns, Charlie Fox's fly, tied with a fluorescent orange body, is somewhat brighter than the average Sulfur pattern, but is a killer most of the time. Charlie's fly is tied with a floss body, but I sometimes use fluorescent orange spun fur. As is done in all my dry flies, the hackle is wrapped over a fur thorax; this helps cushion the hackle, enabling the tier to make a neater hackle collar. Size 16 patterns are the mainstay, although #14s work in streams where the trout do not see many imitations. I get fewer refusals with the #16s. The smaller #18s are rarely needed, but can be the difference between success and failure in certain cases. I tie one pattern called the Fastwater Sulfur, which is intended for heavy water, using a clipped deer-hair body colored pale yellow, along with a much heavier collar of stiff hackle. This fly, when well waterproofed, will float like a cork. Another great variation is the one with cut wings, using pale-blue-dun-hen body feathers as the basis for the wing. These I tie thorax style, with the hackle trimmed on the bottom so the fly floats flush on the surface. This is my "last resort" pattern, used when a particular fish is refusing the other hackle patterns. Recently, I was in one of my favorite Letort meadows at dusk. I had broken off a heavy brown on a poly-wing spinner the week before and was looking for a return engagement. Sure enough the fish was feeding, and I quickly got a hackle pattern over him. There was a boil, but the fly was not sucked under. I tried a few more times, but the fish refused to rise. I waited, and while doing so I tied on one of the cut-wing-thorax ties, with a spread tail and hackle trimmed on the underside. Moments later the fish began to rise again. My first pitch was right, and the fly disappeared in a healthy rise. A heavy-bodied 17-inch brown was fooled completely. Tying descriptions for all ten Sulfur patterns, along with a couple of good nymph and wet-fly imitations, are illustrated in Chapter 13.

Midges

One very important objective of tying any fly smaller than #20 is to offset the hook bend slightly. I do this after I have finished the fly but before I take it from the vise. I push the eye of the hook slightly, giving the desired offset. This greatly helps the qualities of these smaller hooks. The original little gold-plated #28 hooks were offset. As I tied flies on them, I would straighten this offset out to imitate the flat bends of the larger hooks I used. Needless to say, the hooking percentages of the flat #28s were way down. When I offset them again, the number of hooked fish increased dramatically. The Marinaro Midge hooks put out by Partridge have this offset and are one of the better midge hooks on the market, but the flat-bend hooks can be offset just as effectively. Turned-up-eye hooks have never been good hookers for me, even when I use the Turle knot. They make a pretty fly though, so if they work for you, by all means continue with them. Offsetting the bend on down-eyed hooks takes the curse off of the smaller bite created by the down eye, and if you can find ringed-eye midge hooks, so much the better. When you have tied flies as long as I have, to discard accumulated hooks in favor of (possibly) better ones goes against the grain; somewhere in my family there is probably a branch that is Scottish.

The little *Baetis* and *Caenis* mayflies should possibly be included under midges, but I prefer the broader "minutia" description. The little Blue-winged Olive and Minute Rusty Dun are imitative of the *Baetis* mayfly found on most trout streams. The only difference in the tying is that on the rusty dun I use a rusty, cinnamon-colored body, and on the little olive I use a more olive-colored body. The body colors vary slightly from stream to stream, but I don't get too excited if the natural I pick up has a greener body than my imitation. Seldom is the trout that critical as long as the size and shape is right. The little olive mayfly floats along with its wings together and upright, but I prefer a little division on my imitation; I feel this helps balance the fly a little better. If I had only one size to tie, it would be #20 for most streams, but I do tie them in #18, #20, and #22, to be ready for anything.

The little *Caenis*, or *Tricorythodes*, is abundant on many streams throughout the country. It varies slightly in size from one stream to the next, but if you tie it #20 through #28 you will have covered the range sufficiently. Most of the streams I have fished have Tricos most closely imitated by #24. Since the duns emerge mainly at night, and the spinner fall is basically a daylight episode, it stands to reason that the spinner imitation is more important. The Poly-winged Spinner, originated by my good friend Barry Beck, is the best imitation I have found. The use of polypropylene yarn tied as wings was originated by Barry not long after the material became available. I might also mention the Double Trico, or Double Caenis, I devised so I could use a larger hook (#18) and tie two flies to it. This larger hook enabled me to hold on to strong western trout that would have gotten away if a #24 fly had been used. Although I tied Double Olives and Double Rustys as well, the little Double Caenis was, and is, the one I have used most often. I also tie the Trico in both male and female, but I have seldom seen a case where the trout selects one over the other. There are times when a few fish will key in on the *Baetis* and Trico nymphs, so they are important. I'll describe these in more detail in Chapter 13.

Terrestrials

I was literally weaned on the Hard-bodied Ant, as well as on crickets, hoppers, beetles, inchworms, leafhoppers, and locusts. One of the biggest reasons for the terrestrials' popularity is the length of their season. Ants, for instance can be found almost all year; beetles come in a range of sizes and shapes and abound for a number of months; and grasshoppers are early-summer to winter insects. I saw my first ones this year in early June, and I sometimes see them into December, when I'm deer hunting.

While I may have tied some silly flies when I first started tying, the Hard-bodied Ant was my first effective one. I have found that the larger black ants, #10 to #16, are the most effective, while the Hard-bodied Cinnamon Ant seems best in #18 and #20. The late Bob McCafferty is credited with the hard-bodied ties and, according to Charlie Fox, also originated the fur-bodied floaters as well. Bob was also gracious enough to show this lad, at age 12, the correct way to do the double haul, which was practically unheard of in the 1930s. Thanks Bob, for your fly patterns and casting instructions.

As I mentioned, beetles come in a great variety of shapes and sizes. The june bug, for instance, is a long, oval-shaped beetle, and the Japanese beetle is rounder. I try to have some of each in my box. The minute beetles are all tied in a slightly oval shape. Did you know that the lightning bug is a beetle? Trout see numbers of these during the summer, and an imitation with a fluorescent yellow body and a deer-hair back can be very effective. Another good pattern is the Schwiebert Letort Beetle. This tie, originally designed to imitate the Japanese beetle, was patterned after the Jassid-style tie with cock ring-necked pheasant head and neck feathers used as a wing. On the larger ties (#14, #16, and #18) two mated feathers were used, and only one feather was used for the smaller hook sizes. Head cement originally was used on the feathers, which were then trimmed in a broad oval. I now use vinyl cement or flexament to coat the feathers.

Dear to my heart are the Letort Hopper and the Letort Cricket. Although there are numerous hopper and cricket patterns around, I have never felt the necessity of carrying them except on occasion. Call me biased, but they're my babies and I love 'em. If I had only one terrestrial pattern, it would be the Letort Cricket. Even in the West, where hoppers grow big, the smaller ones have worked for me. If you listen to some experts, you must tie up a great bunch of #6s, #8s, and #10s, but pay a little attention to this lowly one too, and tie up some #12s to #18s. You'll be surprised. My favorite size is the #14 2XL for both hopper and cricket. There is great variation in surface tension from stream to stream, much of which is attributed to impurities. On the clean western waters the hoppers sink lower, but don't think all hoppers and crickets float with only their heads out. On the Letort and the Yellow Breeches, for instance, the flies and fly line ride much higher than on other streams. In western waters, even a floating line will need some dressing help on the tip if it is to stay afloat.

Underwater Imitations

My fishing wouldn't be complete without some underwater imitations such as the minnows, sculpins, cress bugs, crayfish, and freshwater shrimp. These and some general-purpose nymphs make up about ninety percent of my underwater flies.

In the past I tied a simple nymph made from mink or weasel fur with guard hair left in. I would rib this with fine gold wire and weight it slightly. This fly suggested not only the scud, or freshwater shrimp, but also the cress bug. I still use the pattern occasionally, and have had success with it.

The original flat-bodied Shenk Cress Bug was devised by using the previously obscure fur-loop method of tying, and once this fuzzy chenille-type fly was completed it was trimmed in a broad, flat shape suggestive of the sow bug or cress bug. Today, the dubbing loop is commonly used as a tying method for various patterns. The original cress-bug ties were medium gray muskrat fur. I also tie other shades, like medium brown olive, and use a mixture of other furs, such as mink and muskrat, to give a dunnish, tannish, nondescript shade that is very effective. Again, I like to weight these slightly so they enter the water and begin to sink immediately. These weighted ones also do great when the fish are holding deep in three to four feet of water.

White marabous are among my favorite streamers. I use them from #4 to #16. One of my favorite sizes has been the little #12 on a 3XL Sproat hook. Lately, my shaped-fur body marabou-tail streamer has been responsible for many large trout. Harry Murray, of Virginia smallmouth fame, swears by the white one he calls Shenk's White Streamer for Old Dominion smallmouths.

My other minnow pattern, the Shenk Sculpin, or Old Ugly, has accounted for more large trout than any other pattern. The all-black version, tied on a #6 2X, or #8 3X hook is one of my favorites. I'm not one to keep records of my fishing stories, so I really don't know the number of trout I have taken on the Old Ugly over the years, but since I already mentioned one of the Yellow Breeches browns of the season, I'll only mention my two best Letort fish. One was a hook-jawed male, not quite 22 inches long, taken just before dark; the other, taken in mid-morning, was exactly 2 feet long. Both were taken on black Old Ugly sculpins.

Bear in mind that one would have to spend countless hours fishing to use all the patterns, styles, and sizes of flies available. But, come to think of it, why not?

Chapter 13

TYING *Special* TECHNIQUES

This chapter refers to tying the flies I have mentioned throughout this book. I give my preferred hook sizes and styles, but a similar hook from another hook maker can be substituted. Over the years I have usually used Mustad brand hooks because they are readily available; however, I have used the Tiemco hooks of Japan, the Partridge and Sealey hooks of England, and the VM hooks of France. I am enamored with the Japanese hooks, with their fine points and tiny flattened barbs. The temper of modern hooks is terrific. I once caught over twenty-five trout on a Sulfur tied on a #16 Partridge Captain Hamilton hook; the fly, though battered, is still serviceable. In releasing that many trout, a tiny fine-wire hook can be bent out of shape quite often, but if the temper is poor, the hook will break after the second or third fish. Inserted is a chart showing hook comparisons between Mustad, Tiemco, and Partridge. Personal choice dictates which hook you use for a particular fly. I still experiment to a certain extent.

Hook Comparison Chart

Mustad	Tiemco	Partridge	Remarks
94840	5210	L3A	Dry Fly
94833	5230	LHA	Dry Fly, 3X fine
94836	100	E6A	Dry Fly, 1X short, ringed eye
3906	3679	63A	Sproat Bend, Nymph
3906B	3761	H1A	Sproat Bend, 1X long
9671	5262	L2A	2X long, good cricket, hopper hook
9672	5162	–	3X long, streamer, terrestrial
79580	300	D4A	4X long, streamer, sculpins

The list could go on and on and on, but this is a start. Now on to the fly patterns. We may as well start with the Sulfur.

Sulfur Dry Fly Patterns

Hook all patterns #1 to #10 Mustad 94840, and #16 and #18 to the 94833

Letort Sulfur Dun

Wing:	none	**Body:**	cream thorax and abdomen
Tail:	cream hackle barbules	**Hackle:**	cream or buff over thorax

Sulfur Dun (Charles Fox)

Wing:	cream hackle tips tied upright, spread slightly	**Body:**	cream or pale-yellow dyed fox fur
Tail:	palest blue dun hackle barbules	**Hackle:**	palest blue dun

147

Sulfur Dun (Ed Shenk)

Wing:	none	**Body:**	cream for abdomen, orange for thorax
Tail:	stiff cream hackle barbules	**Hackle:**	buff, light ginger, and cream hackles (one of each)

Note: Tie the hackles over the thorax, but spread so the orange shows through.

Sulfur Dun Thorax (Vince Marinaro)

Wing:	pale blue dun body feathers shaped with wing-cutter	**Body:**	cream for abdomen and thorax
Tail:	pale blue dun tied in an upward angle to the body	**Hackle:**	pale blue dun tied crisscross under wing

Cut-Wing Sulfur Dun

Wing: Pale blue dun body feathers shaped with wing-cutter

Body: cream or pale yellow for thorax and abdomen

Tail: brown bucktail, split into V shape

Hackle: buff or cream tied behind and in front of wing

Note: Cut a wide V from the bottom so the body of the fly will ride flush with the water's surface.

Harvey Sulfur (George Harvey)

Wing: cream hackle tips

Body: cream fur

Tail: cream hackle barbules

Hackle: mixed cream and bright orange (2 cream, 1 orange)

Fastwater Sulfur (Ed Shenk)

Wing:	none	**Body:**	tan (or dyed pale yellow) deer hair, clipped short
Tail:	tan deer hair	**Hackle:**	stiff buff, tied full with three feathers

Fox Spinner (Charles Fox)

Wing:	none	**Body:**	fluorescent orange floss
Tail:	pale blue dun hackle fibers	**Hackle:**	pale blue dun

Spentwing Sulfur Spinner

Wing: cream hackle tied short

Tail: cream hackle barbules tied into V shape

Body: blended tan fur with a dash of orange

Hackle: (used as wing)

Poly-wing Sulfur Spinner (Barry Beck)

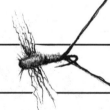

Tail: tan bucktail tied in a wide V

Wing: poly yarn tied spent (pale blue dun)

Body: bright orange (or cinnamon) for abdomen, thorax, head

Hackle: none

Sulfur Nymphs and Wet Flies

Note: I prefer pale yellow thread for these. Hook patterns
Mustad 3906, #16

Sulfur Nymph (Schwiebert)

Tail:	mottled wood-duck fibers	**Wing Cases:**	brown mottled turkey
Abdomen:	rabbit and fox, mixed	**Legs:**	brown partridge fibers
Thorax:	dark brown fur	**Thread:**	black

Note: Rib the abdomen with brown thread.

Little Marryat Wet Fly

Tail:	pale ginger hackle fibers	**Wing:**	pale starling matched-quill sections
Body:	cream and orange fur, mixed	**Hackle:**	pale ginger hen hackle

Light Cahill Wet Fly

Tail: barred wood duck short

Body: cream fur

Wing: barred wood duck

Hackle: cream or light ginger

Terrestrials

Shenk's Letort Hopper

Hook: Mustad 9671, 9672, #6 to #18

Body: yellow spun fur, cream, tan, or orange (you can substitute Fly Rite)

Wing: section of mottled tan turkey feather, folded and tied flat, with the tip trimmed to a broad V, also, tan poly yarn (dark markings with felt tip pen can be used)

Hackle: swept back tips of tan deer hair from the head, trimmed on the underside

Head: spun tan deer hair (trim to shape)

Shenk's Letort Cricket

Hook:	same as hopper		in a broad V (or use black poly yarn)
Body:	black fur dubbing, spun fur, or black Fly Rite	**Hackle:**	black-dyed deer hair tips from head
Wing:	black-dyed goose-quill section, tied flat and trimmed	**Head:**	spun and trimmed black deer hair

---

Fur Ant (black or cinnamon)

Hook:	Mustad 94840, or Partridge Captain Hamilton, #14 to #28		match body, tied dry-fly style in center 1/5 of hook shank; clip a broad V in the underside
Body:	black or cinnamon dubbed fur tied in rounded oval on rear 2/5 of hook	**Head:**	black or cinnamon fur dubbed on forward 2/5 of hook shank
Hackle:	black or ginger to		

Note: You don't need one of each size. I suggest #14, #16, #20, #24, and #28 in black, and #18, #22, and #28 in cinnamon.

Chauncy Lively Deer-hair Ant

Hook: Mustad 94840, #10 to #20

Body: black deer hair tied down with tips extending to rear of hook. The thread is brought to the center of the hook and the deer hair is pulled forward to the center of the hook and tied down. Wrap thread over deer hair to hook eye, then bring thread back to center of hook, pull deer hair back and tie down at center of hook, creating the forward body bulge. Half-hitch or whip-finish thread at the ant's waist. Pick out three hairs on each side for legs and clip off the rest. Add thinned goop or vinyl cement to the hair to strengthen it.

Crowe Beetle

Hook: Mustad 94840, #10 to #22

Note: This fly is tied the same as the Deer-hair Ant, except there is only one body bulge from the hook bend to the eye. Clip off the excess to form a head. Coat the fly with vinyl cement or goop for additional strength.

George Harvey's Clipped-hair Beetle

Hook: Mustad 94840, #10 to #20

Body: brown or black deer hair spun and tied bass-bug style, clipped flat on the bottom and oval on the top with a broad oval silhouette

---

Marinaro Jassid

Hook: Mustad or Partridge dry-fly model, #16 to #28

Body: fur dubbing palmered with matching hackle color; colors can be black, green, brown, ginger; trim the hackle top and bottom

Wing: jungle-cock "nail" (neck feather) tied flat and extended slightly beyond the hook bend; coat the wing with vinyl cement for added durability

Schwiebert's Letort Beetle

Hook: Mustad dry-fly style, #16 to #28

Body: dark for dubbing palmered with matching hackle; hackle clipped top and bottom

Wing: Matching pair of ring-necked pheasant iridescent neck

feathers laid one on top of the other and cemented together with vinyl cement; when dry, they are trimmed to a rear-drop shape; lay wing flat on top of the hook and tie it down

House Fly

Hook: Mustad 94838, #16 to #18

Body: dark gray fur dubbing, tied full

Hackle: three turns of dark dun or black hackle, trimmed on the bottom

George Harvey's Inchworm

Hook: Mustad 9671 or 9672,
#14 to #18

Body: chartreuse deer hair
tied and spun
bass-bug style and
trimmed close

Sinking Inchworm

Hook: Mustad 9672 or
3906B, #12 to #16

Body: chartreuse wool tied
cylindrically and
ribbed with clear 3X
or 4X monofilament

Seventeen Year Locust

Hook: Mustad 9671, #8 to #10

Body: burnt orange dubbing fur tied very full, or, preferably, burnt orange deer hair trimmed very full, flat on bottom

Wing: blue dun hackle tips tied in a narrow V, or a broad body feather tied flat, coated with vinyl cement, and trimmed to a delta-wing shape with rounded wing tips

Hackle: orange, clipped on bottom

Head: large, rounded, and clipped orange deer hair

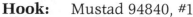

Bumblebee

Hook: Mustad 94840, #10

Body: alternating bands of yellow and black deer hair clipped full

Wing: blue dun hackle tips

Hackle: black, three or four turns

Head: black deer hair, trimmed full

Yellow Jacket

Hook: Mustad 94840, #16 to #18

Body: alternating bands of yellow and black fur dubbing

Wing: blue dun hackle tips

Hackle: two or three turns of black hackle, trimmed on the bottom

Head: black fur dubbing

Hard-bodied Ant (McCafferty)

Hook: Mustad 3906B, #10 to #20

Body: created by wrapping the tying thread (brown or black) into a rounded bulge on the rear 2/5 of the hook, leaving the middle 1/5 open, then wrap another bulge on the front 2/5 of the hook; give bulges a few coats of lacquer, until they are smooth and shiny; when the body is dry, add the hackle (two turns) in the middle of the hook shank and tie off

Minute Dry Flies

Trico Spinner

Thread: black

Hook: Marinaro Midge, #20 to #24

Tail: three long cream hackle fibers or three white hairs from a deer tail (spread these wide)

Abdomen: white for female, black for male

Thorax: black fur behind and in front of the spent wings

Wing: poly-wing material tied spent

Note: On hooks #20 and #22 tie the body the same length as for a #24.

Trico Dun

Thread: black

Hook: same as spinner

Tail: blue dun hackle fibers

Body: dirty cream fur

Hackle: pale blue dun, about three turns

Wing: none

Little Olive (Baetis, Thorax Tie)

Thread: brown

Hook: Mustad 94840, #18 or #20

Tail: bronze blue dun

Body: brown olive fur

Hackle: blue dun (medium) tied over fur thorax and trimmed on the bottom for a flush float

Wing: tiny cut-wings of pale blue dun body feathers

Little Rusty Dun

Same as above, except body is of rusty-colored fur.

No Name

Thread: black

Hook: #18 to #28

Tail: none

Body: light green muskrat dubbing

Hackle: three turns of grizzly

Wing: none

Double Trico Spinner

Thread: black

Hook: Mustad 94840, #18

Tail: three white hairs from a deer tail, spread wide

Body: same as standard Trico spinner

Wing: spent polypropylene (white); make the completed fly on the rear half of the hook, then repeat another fly on the forward half of the hook; the front fly does not require a tail

Double Olive, Double Rusty

Thread: bronze blue dun

Body: olive fur or
rusty-colored fur

Wing: pale blue dun
polypropylene tied
spent; tie two flies,
one in front of the
other, on the hook
shank; fly will have
one tail, one body,
one pair of wings, a
second body and a
second pair of wings

Other Nymphs

Ed Shenk Cress Bug

This was the original fur-loop trimmed-body fly, predating the minnow and sculpin series.

Thread: gray or olive,
prewaxed

Hook: Mustad 3906B, #12
to #20

Body: muskrat, mink, or
otter fur, straight
colors or blended;
form a fur of
dubbing, loop, wrap
solidly to head of fly,
tie off; trim fur flat
on bottom, shallow
oval top, broad oval
sides

Note: If weighting is desired, use a short strip of fuse wire tied on each size of the hook to be wrapped in.

Big Gray Nymph

Thread:	gray or black	**Body:**	fat muskrat fur, dubbed body
Hook:	Mustad 9671, #6 to #10	**Ribbing:**	fine gold wire
Tail:	a few badger hairs, tied short	**Hackle:**	grizzly hen hackle

Note: I vary this by using grouse hackle on some.

Mink Fur Nymph

Thread:	brown or tan		with guard hairs left in, dub fur fairly full
Hook:	Mustad 3906, #12 to #20		
Body:	natural tan mink fur	**Ribbing:**	gold wire, weight optional

Note: This simple little fly probably suggests a scud or freshwater shrimp.

Midges

Midge Pupa

Thread:	color to match body color		green, rust, black, gray, brown, tan
Hook:	Mustad 94840, #18 to #26	**Ribbing:**	gold wire
Tail:	none	**Thorax:**	slight bulge of fur or few turns of ostrich, about same color as body
Body:	various color furs or poly-II; bright		

Midge Larva

Thread:	color to match body		same blend as pupa
Hook:	Mustad 94840, #18 to #26	**Ribbing:**	gold wire
Body:	various colors fur,	**Abdomen:**	none

Adult Midge

Thread: color to match body

Hook: Mustad 94840, #18 to #28

Body: very thin fur or thread

Wing: cream tied back over body

Hackle: cream, grizzly, pale blue dun, two turns

Note: Nothing beats getting a close look at a midge to see firsthand just what they look like so you have a better idea of how to imitate them. This, of course, holds true with any fly.

The Chewy Flies
(Sculpins and Minnows)

Note: All of the following flies use the fur-loop or dubbing-loop style of tying for the bodies.

Fledermaus
(Jack Schneider—The original chewy fly)

Thread:	black		tie full with fur chenille process; do not trim body
Hook:	#12 2XL, to #1 4XL		
Tail:	none	**Wing:**	eastern gray squirrel, very sparse, not much longer than the length of body
Body:	muskrat fur with guard hairs left in;		

Shenk Minnow Series

Hook sizes #2 to #10, 3X or 4XL

Minnow #1 (Shenk's White Streamer)

Tail: white marabou plume not quite as long as the hook shank

Body: cream or white fox fur tied as a fur

chenille; trim to a minnow shape

Head: black or gray nylon thread; painted eyes optional

Minnow #2:

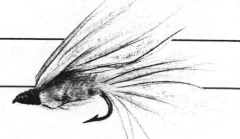

Tail, body, head: same as #1

Wing: white marabou plume

Minnow #3:

Tail, body, head: same as #1

Wing: brown marabou plume

Note: The fur bodies are trimmed to suggest the somewhat oval shape of a minnow. I find the addition of big eyes (painted) adds to the effectiveness of these patterns.

Shenk Sculpin Series

Hook sizes #4 to #10, 2X to 4XL, black thread

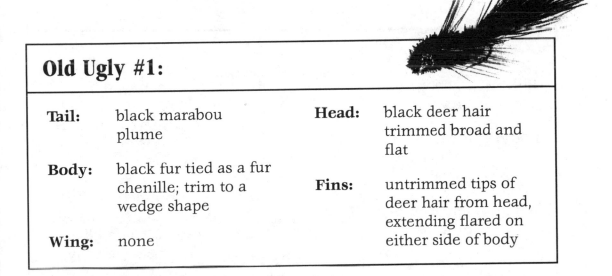

Old Ugly #1:

Tail:	black marabou plume	**Head:**	black deer hair trimmed broad and flat
Body:	black fur tied as a fur chenille; trim to a wedge shape	**Fins:**	untrimmed tips of deer hair from head, extending flared on either side of body
Wing:	none		

Old Ugly #2:

Tail: marabou plume dyed brownish dun

Body: cream fox-fur chenille, trim wedge shape

Wing: marabou plume dyed brownish dun

Head: natural tan, dun, and black deer hair tied to achieve a striped effect; trim broad and flat

Fins: untrimmed tips of deer hair from head extending flared on either side of body

Old Ugly #3:

Same as #2, substituting tan or light brown-olive marabou for tail and wing; black, tan, and brown deer-hair head for striped effect.

Note: Don't use these flies on any leader finer than 4X. Try a 4X for the smaller flies (#8 and #10) and 1X for the largest.

Now you have enough fly patterns to keep you busy for a number of hours. It isn't only the fly pattern you use that determines how great a day you'll have. Learning which flies to use at a particular time and learning how to use them are most important.

PART IV

THE ULTIMATE

FISHING TALE

Chapter 14

The Legend
OF OLD GEORGE

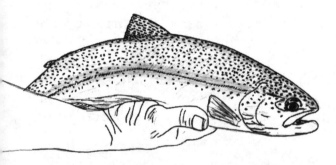

The first rays of morning sun touched the crystal-clear waters of the Letort, one of Pennsylvania's famed limestone trout streams. As if by magic, the surface began to show signs of life. I watched as four trout began to rise upstream. The first was put down by a sloppy cast, but the next two cautiously took the #16 hopper imitation I was using. I caught and released the browns, both about 14 inches long. The fourth wasn't interested.

At one place the water forced itself directly toward a brush pile, faltered momentarily, then continued out and around the obstruction. Again my hopper imitation alighted with a barely audible splat; it drifted four inches and was sucked under by another eager brownie. The splashing rascal was nearly ready for release when it happened—a leg-long shadow emerged from the brush pile, taking the definite form of a monster trout. The 10-inch brown on the end of my line took one last jump before ending up between the jaws of the old leviathan. The line moved slowly back under the brush pile, tightened momentarily, and came free minus the trout.

This took place in 1962, and was my formal introduction to "Old George." I suppose this splendid trout, who became my adversary, began as a tiny native brown in the Letort. We can only guess how fast he grew and how he managed to elude the myriad worms, minnows, spinners, and artificial flies with which anglers tried to tempt him through the years. Quite possibly he was caught and released as a youngster and learned to shun any bait or lure that showed any sign of artificiality.

I fished the pool a number of times during the remainder of that season, but never caught a glimpse of the big fish. I was almost convinced that I had imagined the entire episode.

Then one morning the following season, while fishing the same tiny pool, I spotted a very dark trout in the 20-inch class. About four feet upstream from this trout was a light-colored trout of monstrous proportions – Old George! The 20-incher seemed dwarfed by comparison. I got a little shaky, but drifted a white marabou past the fish. The currents were tricky, so the fly swung wide of the big one and drifted toward Blackie; Blackie went wild as the fly approached, dashing recklessly about the pool. Unhurriedly, the big one swam under the protection of the elodea moss and disappeared. That evening I was back at the pool. I crouched in the grass and drifted a nymph through the hole. A spin fisherman approached on the opposite side of the stream.

"Doin' any good?" I asked.

"Had one nice one on farther downstream," he replied.

We chatted a few minutes, while I secretly wished he'd leave. About that time, the big trout and the black one raced over the moss less than eight inches below the water's surface and swam downstream.

"Did you see those waves?" the spin fisherman cried.

"How could I miss them?" I replied casually. "Those darn big suckers have been racing around for the past hour."

"Oh," he replied. "I thought it was a trout." After a few more words of light conversation, he moved on upstream.

I did a lot of thinking about those trout that night. For one thing, I believed the reason I got so close to them in the morning was that I had been able to approach with the sun at my back, so they were somewhat blinded on that side. I've also seen enough large trout in resting positions to realize that you have to practically put the fly in front of their faces before they'll hit it. I was up early the next morning, fishing elsewhere on the stream, finding it nearly impossible to wait the hour until the sun would be high enough to be to my advantage when I approached the hole.

Eight-thirty finally came, and I slowly eased up to Old George's resting spot. There was Blackie again, with Old George about four feet upstream from him. I judged the spot where the fly should hit to drift down to the big one. It landed in the right spot, but drifted over his back. I added a little bit of strip lead to the 4-pound tippet and cast again. This time the white marabou traveled just right, and as it approached Old George's nose he opened his mighty jaws and inhaled it. I struck, and all hell broke loose. Old George headed for the protection of a big brush pile just a few feet upstream from his resting spot. By shifting my rod, I was able to swing him in a circle away from the logs. I was using a tiny fiberglass rod, 5½ feet long, with a Hardy Featherweight reel filled with Cortland DT4F fly line.

After the third circle, Old George straightened out and headed downstream at a terrific rate – no jumping, just a ninety-mile-per-hour dash. I was rooted to the spot, and the tiny reel gave off a high-pitched shriek. I was holding too hard, putting way too much pressure on the little rod. It was bent almost ninety degrees above the handle, and straight the rest of the way out to the tip. As the monster sought refuge under the edge of a large bed of elodea weed, the leader broke away. I must have been holding my breath, because at that point I exhaled audibly.

I reeled in and saw that the line-to-leader connection had broken. Old George had all ten feet of my tapered leader. I quickly but quietly eased fifty feet downstream, to a point just opposite where Old George was hiding. I placed my rod tip into the water, raised it, and noticed the leader draped over it. With shaking hands I made a hasty line-leader connection, tested it, reeled up the slack line, and felt the weight of the fish. He was still on!

"Man", I thought, "with luck like this, that fish is mine!"

Old George had a different idea though, and took off downstream again. This time I stumbled and splashed after him, but was quickly outdistanced. I could tell where he was by the wake he was making; then he must have passed around one of the few exposed rocks in the Letort because the line suddenly went dead.

"He's sulking," I muttered, but I knew differently.

I walked downstream, reeling line as I went, but when the leader came in sight I knew the fish was gone. I was disappointed at losing the big trout, but then, here was a real challenge. Often, the taking of a trophy is a case of being in the right place at the right time. Although I already knew the right place, when was the right time?

I spied on Old George often enough after that to learn a few things about his habits. I'm convinced that a big trout doesn't have to feed every day, and Old George sort of bore that out. Just as darkness was setting in and the fireflies were beginning to twinkle over the meadows, Old George would move out of his home pool, swimming swiftly downstream and leaving a terrific wake. The waves would subside about seventy-five yards downstream from the hot pool, and then Old George would disappear until just after daylight and then swim swiftly upstream to the home pool again. This baffled me because this water is shallow and contains only a few open channels. The rest of the streambed is literally choked with elodea, and the movement of even a fingerling trout is quickly apparent. I spent hours fishing, and even watched all night for some sign of Old George, but could not get a tumble; at daybreak that big trout would streak upstream once again for his daytime resting place. I used all my pet night flies and never got so much as a follow.

Occasionally, I would catch trout up to 21 inches long from this stretch of water. One dark night, after a late afternoon thunderstorm, I fished from the home pool down to the feeding pool and landed four trout, all longer than 18 inches. These were all released – it was Old George or nothing this season. I even used various baits at night, easing them into the area he traveled while feeding. I'd fish a big, soft crayfish or a juicy minnow and just let it rest all night in one spot, keeping low in the grass so the big boy wouldn't get wise, but it was all to no avail. Old George just wasn't your ordinary large trout, which is a sucker for a large fly after dark.

In addition to his evening habits, I could usually see Old George resting in the home pool between eight o'clock and noon. I'd try something different nearly every time I fished, but one drift past the fish was all I'd get before he would swirl back under the elodea or charge up under the brush pile. The black trout was still skittery, so I decided to try to get it out of the way. One nervous fish in the pool was enough! The black one finally took a tiny weasel-fur nymph late one afternoon and was played downstream and released. I never saw it again.

Evidently Old George had been stung by a minnow fisherman previously, because minnows made him extremely edgy. Thinking he might be leader-shy, I tried drifting a minnow past him on the end of a 5X leader, but his reaction was the same. It wasn't the leader, it was the bait. I fashioned a big weighted nymph, similar to a crayfish, out of wildcat fur, on a #2 hook. I had hit the right spot for a decent drift so many times I could do it blindfolded. This try was no different; the nymph sank immediately and eased its way toward Old George's snout. The big jaws opened, then closed, on the fly, and I was into him again.

This time I was ready for the big run downstream and got below him after running down the bank about fifty yards. Immediately he reversed course and headed home. I put on the pressure but barely slowed him down. My leader was heavy this time and I was holding my own when the fly pulled out and scraped the fish on the side as it came back toward me. Old George went home. I reeled in and found two large scales on the point of the hook. Later, from a scale reading with a 10-power glass, I estimated the fish to be eight years old.

I often wonder what dear old Mrs. Otto thought when she saw that crazy Ed Shenk running down along the bank, rod held high, stumbling as he went.

"Now I know everything about him except how to catch him," I muttered.

Episode three, a few days later, was short and sweet. He took a muskrat nymph this time. *Z-z-zip* – just that quickly he was under the brush pile, and I was nervously nursing a broken 7-pound leader.

Old George was not stupid. It took many days, many stealthy approaches, and many casts to get him to take one snap at the fly. On the days when the approach was a little sloppy or the cast a little suspicious, the big brown would be in hiding before I could bat an eye.

By now the fish was becoming an obsession with me. I was making daily runs to the Letort, a five-minute drive from my home in Carlisle. When the alarm would awaken me before daylight, I'd think, "Today is the day," and after a strong belt of coffee I'd be on my way. Stealthily, I would fish Old George's feeding area, watching for some sign of big-fish activity. At 5:45 I'd see the big wake as Old George made a run for his resting pool, then I would fish elsewhere on the stream until the sun rose to the right position.

One time I joined Dr. Dale Coman of Philadelphia and Bar Harbor for a few hours on the stream. We began fishing just below the old Reading Railroad bridge. Watching the water, we would put an ant, hopper, or cricket over a fish when it rose to one of the various terrestrials common to the meadows in summer. Dale had taken a few decent browns by the time we reached the Otto farmhouse. At that time the elderly Ottos were still farming and pasturing cattle in the streamside acreage. There was an electric fence strung out over the water, so I cautioned the good doctor and pointed out one stray wire that I had touched before without being shocked. "This one's not hot," I said, "but be careful of the others." Dale liked to wade wet in the summertime, and as I crawled under the cold wire with no problem I heard a *zap* and a heavy splash. Wheeling around, I saw a pale, very still, Doctor Coman lying on his back in the water. I dragged him to the bank and revived him. Needless to say, I was very apologetic because I realized my rubber waders had grounded me. Of course, he had no such protection.

The home pool for Old George was the one directly in front of Otto's farmhouse. "How would you like to see Old George?" I asked. As luck would have it, the great brown was out in the open. "Give him a try," I said. "Not on your life," Dale replied, "if I fished for Old George now you would probably finish the electrocution job on me!"

Another fishing episode came a few days later during a heavy downpour. The water got yellow-muddy after a short time and I headed for the tiny channel of water between Old George's feeding spot and his resting spot. I had the feeling that the old boy might be out snooting around for a little extra tidbit or two, so, slowly and methodically I probed every inch of the little channel to make certain that if the big fish was about, I'd get the big juicy worm close enough for him to see it. On one drift the line stopped, and I could see and feel the heavy tug associated with a large trout; little ones go *tick, tick, tick* when they work on a bait. I set the hook and felt the tremendous surge of a big fish. "Old George," I muttered, but it wasn't to be. Just inches beside the deep-boring fish, a heavy, steady wave ended in the home pool. I knew what that meant! Shortly, I landed a heavy-bodied 5-pound brown; after a short admiring session I watched this fish disappear into the murky water. I can picture these two great trout feeding side-by-side and Old George saying to his companion, "Hey, look at that super worm coming down. Go ahead, it's all yours." As I've always said, there's a time to put all selfishness aside, and I guess this was one of those times.

The fourth hook-up was again short and sweet. I was able to get a #4 Wildcat Nymph near the old leviathan; it was inhaled, and quickly Old George was up under the logjam. The big bed of elodea near which this great fish rested was overhung, and each time the trout was disturbed it nestled farther back under the bed. I still think this fish would lie in the sun for its healing powers, just as an old person sits in the sun for the same reason. Finally, the trout was so far under the overhang that any normal cast, no matter how close to the bed, would swing too wide. Bear in mind that this fish never moved left or right for a fly. It had to be cast dead-on, and even then there was no guarantee.

I had been criticized for using small rods in my fishing, and was told by Ross Trimmer that if I used a larger, more powerful rod I would have landed that "damn" fish a long time ago. Therefore, I brought out a Uslan five-strip 8½-foot bamboo Powerhouse. I wanted a longer rod so I could poke its tip in the water and get the fly closer to the fish. I was using 15-pound-test leader and approached close enough, by wading deeper, so my big marabou would swing under the elodea and begin to brush the nose of the old brown. I could tell that the fish was becoming annoyed because it started to periodically shake its head, just like an animal with an annoying insect flitting in its face. Finally, the fish got so annoyed and angry that, with a great snap, the fly was inhaled. I reared back on the rod, and the fight was on. On for about one second, that is, until Old George swiftly plowed his way into the blasted logjam. "I got you this time you old bastard," I shouted. "You'll never break that leader." In a flash, the remnants of the leader drifted free from the logs. The end looked like it had been cut with a knife.

I failed to see the big boy during the next few days, so I became alarmed. Had someone speared him? Had I bothered him so much that he had moved to a new location? I finally decided the latter was the case. A friend of mine, aware of my battles with Old George, saved me from what could have been a lengthy search.

"I know where that big one is that you've been fishing for," said Dr. "Howdy" Hoffman of Chambersburg. "He's living in the deep hole under the leaning tree about 100 yards below Otto's farmhouse."

That sly old rascal had moved to a hole at the lower end of his "beat." Now, instead of dropping downstream to feed, he cruised upstream to the exact same feeding area. I had to close one chapter on the habits of Old George and begin a new one.

As usual, Old George fed at dusk, dropping back down at daybreak or shortly thereafter. It's surprising just how much this fish knew about his surroundings. He knew every bush and tree that grew along the stream. For instance, for three mornings in a row I saw the big wake move downstream at exactly 5:45. On the fourth morning I was in a position to intercept him, when, right on schedule, the action started. I was hidden motionless in the tall grass where Old George would pass four feet in front of me. I still wasn't quite sure of the size of the fish, so this was going to be a good opportunity to get a look. As the fish passed me, he must have recognized something wrong, because he bolted and headed for home at great speed.

The following morning I was back, trying to coax a strike with a Fledermaus streamer, with no action at all. I moved below the new hideout, and only then did the great fish make a dash for home. What a dash it was! The great wake, seeming to splash water on both banks at once, finally subsided.

I had trouble from the beginning fishing the new location. Over the years I had caught a half-dozen big trout from that pool, but when Old George was hiding under the bank I could never get him to come for anything. When he was sunning himself it was nearly impossible to approach without another trout darting around and warning him. The pool was so shaded that there was only one period of the day when it was hit by the sun—between 3:30 and 4:30 P.M. At that time, day after day, I would give it a try. Generally, the big fish would bolt on the first cast. Once, I tried at dusk during a warm summer rain, fishing a long line from upstream and bracketing the pool with casts. I caught and released five trout from 14 to 20 inches long, but never saw Old George.

The 1963 season slowly came to a close, and I had one quick chance on the final day. I drifted a black marabou toward the big fish. He mouthed it and then spat it out before I tensed to strike. A quick flap of the tail sent him into hiding. All winter I kept watching for my trout, but never saw him. The wild duck were so thick on the surface that the water was always cloudy. Once I saw a tremendous trout in one of the watercress ponds about a half-mile upstream. It was December, and I felt perhaps Old George had moved upstream to spawn.

In April of 1964 I was on the Letort one day at 5 A.M., the legal starting time. I didn't see a sign of Old George. Later the same day I took a run to Yellow Breeches Creek and killed a pair of 3-pound rainbows, but my mind was on the big one in the Letort. Had he moved? Had he died over the winter? I wasn't sure. It was the next month before I saw him again. He came out from under the bank and shot upstream at a rapid pace. I managed one cast, but it was the same old story. The fly hadn't drifted to within three feet of the big one before he darted into the tree roots under the overhanging bank. I believe the old boy saw me and associated the fisherman with the fly. It's odd how you tend to overlook simple little details in fishing. Each time I had tried to approach the big fish I had done so in an upright position, depending upon the sun to shield my presence.

At 4:30 on the afternoon of May 14, I made another try for Old George. Before I got to his resting place I soaked my white marabou so it would submerge as soon as it hit the water. I also pinched a tiny bit of strip lead to the eye of the hook to take the fly down more quickly. I approached the hole on hands and knees for a change, and peeped over the bank; the grass was knee-high, so I was totally concealed. He was there! I was using a 10-foot leader tapered to a 2X. I stripped it and two feet of line through the guides of my tiny rod, a 5-foot fiberglass weighing one ounce, which I had made myself. A slight movement of the rod sent the fly to the tiny current that would drift it past Old George. When the marabou was two feet in front of him his entire body became alert. I was excited because I knew the fish was going to take the fly. I pumped the rod tip once, and the marabou quivered like Fatima going into her belly dance. A pair of gaping jaws opened and engulfed the fly. I struck and stood up at the same time.

Old George shook his head like a punch-drunk fighter, turned, and headed downstream. I put on all the pressure I dared, but the fish fought relentlessly. I jumped into the water to follow him – to Carlisle, if necessary. The big bruiser got alarmingly close to a log obstruction and freedom – then I tried a new maneuver. I gave him lots of slack line, hoping he would turn and head upstream for home. He did, and the hook held. The marabou was on a hook with a pinched-down barb, so I was fortunate that it didn't drop out of his mouth. As the fish passed me coming upstream I tightened the line again and resumed the battle. Three times I guided the trout halfway around the pool, but then he made it to the protection of the overhanging bank. I was aware that the line was still tight.

Old George stayed under the bank for about four minutes, but I kept pressure on him until he bolted again, this time upstream. Surprisingly, the line became untangled, so I quickly climbed the bank to follow him upstream. The trout came to rest at the upper end of the pool, shaking his head from side to side. I could see he was tired; his mouth was opening and closing, and his gills were flared. I put pressure on him and forced him closer to me. Now that I had him wallowing within netting distance, I was faced with a new problem. I knew my net was big enough, but I wondered how I could get him into it head-first. I made a false move, and Old George made a last-chance surge toward freedom. Slowly, I worked the fish back into position, eased the net into the water, and led the trout into it. Old George was at long last mine! When I lifted my prize from the net, my #4 Silver Garland Marabou had already dropped out of its mouth.

I went back to the car and drove downstream to Charlie Fox's meadow. Charles, Doc Coman, and Chuck Kisinger were there. After brief congratulations, "Glad" Fox, Charlie's wife, took a few pictures, and we weighed the trout. Old George measured 27¼ inches and weighed exactly 8½ pounds. Not the largest trout from the Letort, but close to it. To top it off, Old George was a lady!

I am pleased that I was finally able to outwit and land Old George; but I get a funny feeling every time I look into the pool the big fish called home. Somehow I still expect to peek over the bank and see the wonderful shape of that great old fish gently finning in the crystal current. I'm sorry that I never again will.

Postscript: The very next time I went fishing I tested my glued-up line-leader splice. This was before epoxy, and the epoxy splice. The connection parted with only a few ounces pull. Could it be that fate just meant for me to have that fish? I think so.

186